IT HAPPENED IN
FLORIDA

T0356449

IT HAPPENED IN

FLORIDA

Stories of Events and People That Shaped
SUNSHINE STATE HISTORY

Third Edition

E. LYNNE WRIGHT

Globe
Pequot   ESSEX, CONNECTICUT

Globe Pequot

An imprint of The Globe Pequot Publishing Group, Inc.
64 South Main Street
Essex, CT 06426
www.globepequot.com

Distributed by NATIONAL BOOK NETWORK

British Library Cataloguing in Publication Information available

Library of Congress Cataloging-in-Publication Data

Names: Wright, E. Lynne, 1931– author.
Title: It happened in Florida : stories of events and people that shaped the Sunshine State / E. Lynne Wright.
Other titles: It happened in series.
Description: Third edition. | Essex, CT : Globe Pequot, [2025] | Series: It happened in | Includes bibliographical references and index.
Identifiers: LCCN 2024042546 (print) | LCCN 2024042547 (ebook) | ISBN 9781493088546 (paperback ; alkaline paper) | ISBN 9781493088553 (epub)
Subjects: LCSH: Florida—History—Anecdotes. | LCGFT: Anecdotes.
Classification: LCC F311.6 .W75 2025 (print) | LCC F311.6 (ebook) | DDC 975.9—dc23/eng/20240923
LC record available at https://lccn.loc.gov/2024042546
LC ebook record available at https://lccn.loc.gov/2024042547

♾️™ The paper used in this publication meets the minimum requirements of American National Standard for Information Sciences—Permanence of Paper for Printed Library Materials, ANSI/NISO Z39.48-1992.

CONTENTS

ACKNOWLEDGMENTS

I owe so much to so many who helped me with the research of this book. I want to thank the reference librarians at the Indian River County Main Library in Vero Beach, who were always so helpful. I also thank the University of Florida College of Medicine, the Indian River County Audubon Society, the Florida State Archives in Tallahassee, and the Sanford L. Ziff Jewish Museum. A million thanks to my considerate and helpful editor, Kate Ayers. Special thanks to my daughter, Wendy, who sacrificed precious time to help me with some of the modern technology that confused her mother. She was always there when two pairs of hands were needed. Finally, I thank my son, Craig, who took time from his busy schedule when my printer stopped working or when I needed to replace parts of something else to keep things going. They are the two best cheerleaders and fixer-uppers anywhere.

PREFACE

Like so many other people, I came to Florida from somewhere else, drawn here by the chance to escape northern winters, not anticipating anything other than sunny days, good boating, and lots of navel oranges. Florida history was the last thing on my mind, but I kept bumping into some of the same names over and over. Henry Flagler, for one. His name seemed to pop up everywhere. There was Flagler Beach, Flagler County, the railroad he built, and his hotels that rivaled the Taj Mahal. His private life, I discovered, was even more interesting.

And what was so special about someone named Osceola? He was a Native American, obviously, but why did I run into his name every time I turned a corner?

Make a trip to the Everglades and inevitably the name Marjory Stoneman Douglas will come up. But she had so much more to her credit than simply being a champion of the Everglades, as if that weren't enough. What a woman!

Slowly, I became hooked. So many fascinating things have happened in Florida. And why not? European history got started on this continent in 1513 in Florida, not on that big rock in Massachusetts in 1620. By that time, St. Augustine already had shops, a church, and a hospital. The Pilgrims were the new kids on the block.

The same climate and sunny days that brought me to Florida have brought other folks, too, from New York, Ontario, Havana, Russia—you name it—some for vacations, others as part-time "snowbirds." Some lucky ones like me have made Florida their year-round home. There's good and bad in that. Being home to so many people from somewhere else keeps things interesting in the Sunshine State, but it can lead to divided allegiances. Some have bodies that tan in this sunny paradise, but their hearts and their families reside somewhere else.

This might have something to do with the well-established Florida tradition: "Take the money and run." Everyone, it seems, wants to take something from Florida. What's taken these days might be happy memories and a pair of "mouse ears," but in the past it included pine-wood forests, egret feathers, Seminole tribal lands, turtle eggs, and alligator skins.

Generally speaking, people don't concern themselves much with Florida history. Instead, they concentrate mainly on what has happened in recent years in the state: the presidential and gubernatorial elections, hurricanes, shark attacks, and games involving the Dolphins, Marlins, Gators, and other popular teams.

Reading Florida history can be comforting. It reminds us that people in the past survived the same things we're facing today. Ads for in-home shelters to ensure safety from bioterrorists after the attacks of September 11, 2001, echoed the backyard bomb shelters hastily built during the Cuban missile crisis. Although they didn't manage to inflict much damage, Nazi saboteurs invaded our shores in 1942, long before the foreign terrorists of 2001. The election of 1876 was no more satisfying to half the nation than the election in 2000, but we survived them both. Will we survive the most recent one? We made it before; we'll do it again.

Floridians will continue putting out the welcome mat, hoping snowbirds, transplants, and tourists, too, will come for the sunshine but also take time to check into the fascinating history of this lovely peninsula. As well as being comforting, finding out what happened in Florida can be fun—a day at the beach, you might say.

1513

Ponce de León's Reception in the New World

From the beginning, immigrants have sometimes received a less-than-warm welcome in the New World. Juan Ponce de León was no exception. In fact, the man who is credited with discovering Florida had such an ignominious debut in America, he spent very little actual time on our soil before fleeing for his life.

Florida's recorded history began with Ponce, a Spanish nobleman who, like other explorers of his day, was unquestionably motivated by a quest for power, riches, and natives to enslave.

The myth of the Fountain of Youth, so firmly attached to Ponce's name, probably started with Indians repeating tales about healing waters told to them by other European explorers. The legend of such a fountain or spring existed in many parts of the world and could be traced to the fabled "water of life" in the Garden of Eden, supposedly located in the Far East. Early Spanish explorers thought America was the Far East, possibly convincing some that the fountain must be somewhere in the New World. Bearing in mind that neither Spaniards nor Indians were bilingual and Spanish explorers needed to periodically replenish their drinking water, it seems logical that requests for "fresh" or "sweet" water could be interpreted as rejuvenating water from a spring or fountain.

The only existing source containing firsthand details of Ponce's journey is a monumental ten-volume work published about 1610. It contains no mention of a Fountain of Youth. The lures of finding gold and conquering new territories were the usual reasons for men to explore strange lands, and there is little reason to doubt these reasons were uppermost in Ponce de León's mind as well.

Ponce had sailed with Christopher Columbus's second voyage to the New World in 1493, when Puerto Rico was discovered. At that time, Ponce remained on the island of Hispaniola to establish a settlement and enslave natives to mine the gold deposits he expected to find. The Spanish king rewarded him with the governorship of eastern Hispaniola (now the Dominican Republic), then the governorship of Puerto Rico. Accordingly, Ponce's wealth increased.

However, during the palace intrigue following Columbus's death, his son, Diego Columbus, claimed all his father's possessions, along with the right to install his own people as governors. Being unceremoniously ousted from his job must have been the irritant that helped energize Ponce to pursue his own discoveries and add to his wealth and prestige.

In 1513, he set out from Puerto Rico with three ships, heading north until he reached what he thought was an island, probably near what is now the city of Melbourne, Florida. Over the years, St. Augustine has claimed to be the spot where the Spaniards landed, dispensing water from its springs to eager tourists, but studies of Ponce's navigation log using modern instruments render this unlikely. Additionally, one can't help but notice that there are no records of tourists enjoying incredibly long life spans after quenching their thirst in St. Augustine.

Since it was the Easter season, *Pascua florida,* and the land "had a very beautiful view of many and cool woodlands," Ponce named it *La Florida,* "Land of Flowers." Under the patent granted him by King Ferdinand, Ponce claimed his discovery for Spain. Heading south, he made a second discovery, although at the time he did not recognize it for what it was.

As Ponce's three vessels followed the coast, it became increasingly difficult to make forward progress despite strong winds in their favor. Gradually, the current became stronger than the wind, causing the ships to regress rather than sail forward. The two caravels nearest land dropped anchor, but the smaller brigantine in deeper waters was unable to anchor. Carried out to sea, it disappeared from sight.

The Spaniards had discovered a "river" fifty to three hundred miles wide in the ocean. Ponce de León's pilot, realizing its significance, made notes for charting a route for ships to be carried on their voyages home, a great boon to Spanish exploration. Today, we call this "river" the Gulf Stream. Even now, large tankers traveling north ride the Gulf Stream to save valuable time.

While his ship lay at anchor awaiting the return of the brigantine, several Indians waved to Ponce from shore. Thinking he had found some likely prospects to mine the riches he expected to find on his "island," Ponce waved back as he began rowing ashore with some men. A sudden flurry of bone-tipped arrows and spears rained down, convincing the Spaniards to await the return of the brigantine from a safer distance.

As they replenished firewood and water near what was later called Jupiter Inlet, they might well have wondered if their ungracious welcome was due to messages carried to the Indians by escaped Caribbean slaves, victims of Ponce de León's suppression of Puerto Rican natives.

After reuniting with their missing ship, Ponce and his men sailed on to the last of the keys, where they feasted on turtles, appropriately naming the islands the Tortugas. Replenishing wood and water again, they sailed north as far as Sanibel Island, where they careened one ship for repairs. As they worked, an Indian shouted in Spanish from a distance, saying his chief would like to trade much gold with them. The wary Ponce only waved back in response, but shortly afterward, Indians in canoes were grabbing the anchor line, attempting to drag Ponce's ship to shore while others began an assault. The Spaniards fought them off and, having had their fill of unfriendly Indians, sailed back to the safety of Puerto Rico.

In his seven-month journey, Ponce had been greeted by hostile natives, was unable to establish a permanent settlement, and, to his great disappointment, had no fabulous wealth to show for his trouble.

Unaware that he had actually discovered the tip of a new continent, he remained in Puerto Rico, accruing wealth to finance more expeditions. Reports of successful discoveries by other explorers tormented him, especially tales of the vast riches Hernando Cortés sent to Spain from his conquest of Mexico.

In 1521, Ponce decided to try again. Armed with documents naming him governor of Florida and intending to establish a colony where he would get his share of the fabulous wealth of the New World, he set out with soldiers, farmers, priests, supplies, cows, and other animals. He anchored off Estero Bay, near Fort Myers Beach, close to where he had been eight years previously.

Whether or not the same Indians recognized him and his party, their greeting was much the same—a fierce attack. An arrow pierced Ponce's armor, wounding him seriously. His men carried him to the ship and hastily departed the Land of Flowers, setting sail for Cuba, where Ponce died of his wounds. His body was returned to Puerto Rico and buried.

Ponce de León died unaware of the true significance of the "island" he claimed for Spain, or the importance of the great "river" he discovered in the ocean, or even that the Andalusia cattle he took along on the 1521 voyage would be the forebears of modern Florida's thriving cattle industry. He barely set foot on his "island" and never glimpsed gold, but he became more famous in ensuing English history books than he did among his Spanish contemporaries.

Florida's first governor would surely be pleased that part of his discovery would one day be known as the Gold Coast, some of the most highly valued property in the richest nation in the world.

1838

Osceola Betrayed

In 1786, Thomas Jefferson loftily proclaimed, "It may be regarded as certain that not a foot of land will ever be taken from the Indians without their consent."

After that, things went downhill.

A treaty signed in 1823, supposedly effective for twenty years and no bargain for Florida's Seminoles to begin with, was violated in 1830 with President Andrew Jackson's signing of the Indian Removal Bill. Then the newest government Indian agent, Wiley Thompson, asked the Seminoles to sign yet another treaty, which would move them to undesirable lands in the West amid other Indian tribes who were their enemies. In response, a charismatic young Seminole named Osceola whipped out his knife, stabbed the treaty on the council table, and snarled, "This is the only treaty I will ever make with the Whites!"

The legend of Osceola had begun.

His name, *Asi Yahola,* corrupted by White men into Osceola, would become one of the most famous of all Indian names. Born about 1803, he denied stories of being part Indian, announcing emphatically, "No foreign blood runs in my veins. I am a pure blood." His mother was Creek, and since Creek and Seminole tribal structure was matrilineal, he was a member of his mother's clan, justified in claiming descent and inheritance from her.

Although he was not a chief by heredity and his time of influence was brief, he not only led his own people but was destined to become the idol of many White people.

After the treaty-stabbing incident, Osceola seldom missed an opportunity to show contempt for White men's treaties. He shot Agent Thompson in 1835, causing a further rift in American-Seminole relations and sparking the Second Seminole War. Thompson grew to hate Osceola so much that, during one acrimonious session in his office, the agent had him jailed with his wrists bound tightly enough that scars formed. Osceola, nearly insane with anger, raged for hours, then plotted revenge. Released six days later, still seething inwardly, he pretended to be remorseful. His performance must have been convincing because the grateful Thompson gave him a custom-made rifle—a major error on his part, as it turned out.

Some time later, when Thompson and a companion were out for a stroll, Osceola, brandishing his new rifle, stepped from behind some trees. After killing both men, Osceola scalped Thompson and, as payback, cut his scalp into pieces, giving each Indian in his group a souvenir.

Newspapers reported Osceola's escapades, including his badgering of government troops and outsmarting of several generals. He watched his enemies from a distance, marveling at their clumsy, noisy maneuverings, so unlike the Indians' silent movements through the forests.

But both Seminoles and White settlers tired as the feud dragged on. Food, energy, and ammunition were running low, and any trust they ever had in each other had run out.

Finally, Osceola agreed to meet for peace talks with the latest White commander, General Thomas S. Jesup, under a flag of truce. Like all Seminoles, Osceola regarded the white flag as almost sacred. But once inside the camp, his party was surrounded, and he was knocked on the head, bound, and thrown into a cell.

As word of the betrayal spread, the entire nation and even other nations were outraged and disgusted. Congress investigated Jesup, ending up evenly divided for and against him. His name became synonymous with treachery, and he spent much of the rest of his life defending his actions.

Osceola had been suffering from intermittent fevers, now thought to have been malaria. He was tired, ill, and defeated. His two wives and one child were permitted to join him in prison at Fort Marion in St. Augustine, the oldest fort in the United States. The man who had lived easily in a vast forest and bathed in clean rivers spent the next five weeks in the overcrowded fort, experiencing a recurrence of his illness exacerbated by poor hygiene and an infestation of fleas. (Scientists examined strands of Osceola's hair that were among artifacts passed to descendants of his attending physicians. Tests indicated that Osceola suffered from head lice which, untreated, could also cause fevers and chills.)

As more Indians were captured, the prison became even more crowded, and sanitation deteriorated. A measles outbreak followed by a prison escape contributed to the decision to move the prisoners to a safer site. Fort Moultrie in Charleston, South Carolina, was chosen. The incarcerated Indians would be removed from their homeland after all.

During his imprisonment, Osceola was attended by the Fort Marion physician Dr. Frederick Weedon, a colonel in Andrew Jackson's army who had settled in St. Augustine. Osceola had developed acute tonsillitis, a serious condition in those times. Trust between doctor and patient grew to the point that, when the Indians found out they were to be moved, Osceola asked that Weedon accompany them.

Though something of a celebrity and well treated by his captors, Osceola's life ebbed. Dr. Weedon visited him every few hours and consulted with his friend, Dr. Benjamin Strobel, professor of anatomy in Charleston. Both physicians did everything they could, but Seminole medicine men who were present prevented several measures the doctors felt would benefit the patient. Dr. Weedon recorded in his diary that Osceola asked "that his Bones Should be permitted to remain in peace and that I should take them To Florida & place them where I Knew they would not be disturbed."

Early on January 30, 1838, with Weedon present, Osceola asked for his best clothes. He dressed, painted half of his face, hands, and knife handle with red paint—an oath of war—smilingly shook hands all around with Indians and White men alike, laid back grasping his scalping knife, crossed his hands, and died.

Even then, the indignities did not stop. Dr. Weedon, Osceola's best White friend, during a moment alone with the corpse, beheaded the body.

Several theories attempt to explain this bizarre behavior, but none explains it any better than the doctor's great-granddaughter, who said, "Dr. Weedon was an unusual man." While the warrior's body was buried at Fort Moultrie, in Charleston, South Carolina, Dr. Weedon embalmed the head and took it with him when he returned to St. Augustine, keeping it in his home, where he also had his office. His great-granddaughter related that when one of his sons misbehaved, the doctor would hang the embalmed head from the boy's bedpost to teach him a lesson. An unusual man indeed.

Eventually, Weedon gave the head to his son-in-law, Dr. Daniel Whitehurst, who, in turn, sent it to his former professor, Dr. Valentine Mott, a New York City surgeon. White historians think the head was destroyed in a fire at the medical college where Dr. Mott kept specimens. However, Seminoles, citing Mott's statement that he was keeping the head at his home, believe it still exists.

Since the 1930s, Florida and South Carolina have argued intermittently about who should have Osceola's grave. Charleston believes it would become "just another tourist attraction" in Florida. Florida accuses Charleston of "gross neglect" of the grave, citing a 1966 incident when a park guard discovered that someone had been digging at the gravesite. Immediately after the discovery, local police were joined by the Federal Bureau of Investigation and news reporters. By that time, Fort Moultrie National Monument was under the authority of the National Park Service, which began an archeological investigation. The investigation disclosed a headless skeleton still in the grave identified as belonging to Osceola.

Although few outside their families and some historians remember Jesup, Thompson, or Weedon, in the United

States there are three counties, two townships, twenty towns, one borough, one state park, two lakes, a national forest, and a dormitory hall at Florida State University that bear the name of the Seminole warrior Osceola.

Despite his deathbed request, Osceola's bones are still not in their Florida home.

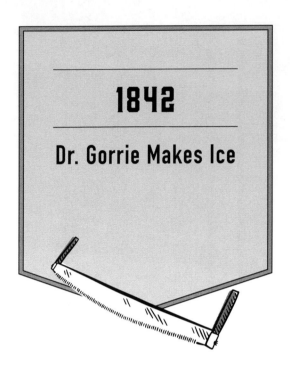

1842

Dr. Gorrie Makes Ice

During the summer of 1841, more than one hundred people died in Apalachicola when the Gulf port town, one of Florida's most important seaports, reeled under the annual recurrence of yellow fever and malaria. One local physician, Dr. John Gorrie, obsessed with learning to control the fevers, worked devotedly, caring for patients in two regional hospitals. The recurrence of the illnesses during months of soaring heat and humidity led him to deduce that the possible cause might be airborne miasmas from decomposing vegetation.

Dr. Gorrie had been the postmaster, city council chairman, treasurer, and mayor while he maintained interests in the Mansion House Hotel, two banks, and the Apalachicola Land Company. He also founded Trinity Church in Apalachicola in the days before he became obsessed with the all-consuming goal of helping people suffering from the fevers. Capitalizing on the goodwill he had earned among his fellow citizens, he constantly harangued them to drain swamps and use mosquito nets to filter from the air the poisons he believed were causing the sicknesses. Whenever he could spare a moment, he shut himself in the laboratory attached to his house, searching for a means to dry and cool the air in his patients' rooms in hopes of controlling their fevers.

Success finally arrived on a June afternoon in 1842. Normally shy and reserved, the doctor recognized that what he had accomplished would have far-reaching effects and, eager to share the news, he rushed to find his friend, Dr. Alvan Chapman, who was mixing prescriptions in his dispensary. Dr. Chapman was one of the few who knew about Gorrie's search for a way of reducing patients' temperatures.

"Well," Dr. Chapman said, "have you found a way to freeze your patients?"

"No, but I've made ice!" was Dr. Gorrie's astounding announcement.

During experiments with cooling air, Gorrie had accidentally produced small blocks of "artificial" ice. Although benefiting patients was always his primary concern, he realized there could be other as-yet undreamed-of possibilities in the making of ice. Someday, he predicted, foods could be frozen solid to preserve them, an improvement over salting, pickling, and drying, which were then the only means of food preservation.

Chapman, a botanist, was excited for his friend. He later assisted him with a demonstration at the Mansion House Hotel, organized by a Monsieur Rosan, a French cotton buyer who lived in Apalachicola during the shipping season.

Since about 1805, New England shipowners had chopped ice from lakes and rivers in the region, loaded it into insulated ships, and sold it to southern cities. The larger cities built huge, insulated vaults to store the blocks of ice. Unfortunately, after stops in Savannah and Charleston, the ships were sometimes empty by the time they reached the docks in Apalachicola. When ships failed to arrive at all, as frequently happened, mint juleps were served warm.

On this occasion, even though no ice ship had been in port for some time, Rosan dazzled his guests with chilled champagne before moving the entire party to Gorrie's laboratory, where the doctor demonstrated his ice-making machine.

The machine consisted of two compressor pumps—one to compress air, the other to expand it—both run by steam, with a storage chamber in between to feed cool air through pipes into patients' rooms. When the cool air passed around a container of water, ice formed.

Properly impressed, the party then proceeded to a room used for fever patients, where, on that sweltering summer evening, the air was delightfully dry, cool, and comfortable. A basin of ice had been suspended from the ceiling with a pipe extending from the basin through a hole in the ceiling to the chimney, allowing air to enter the room. With the doors and windows closed and another pipe at floor level, air entered the room at the ceiling, was cooled by the ice in the basin, and was drawn to the floor where it was discharged to the outside.

The guests were astounded, and the news circulated quickly, though not to everyone's delight. "If the Lord intended ice in Florida, He would have put it there," was one pious man's objection.

Accumulating wealth had never been Dr. Gorrie's ambition; the possibility of eliminating illness and death was always uppermost in his mind. However, Gorrie needed to begin a search for financial backers since his own finances and those of his wife had been exhausted by his research and attempts to launch the manufacture of his invention. The one backer who came forward died suddenly, and by some strange legal twist, Gorrie was declared legally responsible for the backer's debts as well as his own.

His application for a patent was approved in 1851, but in the meantime, as a search for funding went on, a crusade of disparagement began. New England shipowners, aware that Dr. Gorrie's ice machine could spell disaster for their lucrative ice trade, enlisted northern newspapers in a campaign of ridicule. "How could you trust a man who said he made ice in Florida in the summer?" one asked. "If a man could produce this miracle, why couldn't he get financing?" said another.

The scheme worked. No other backer came forth. Dr. Gorrie, desiring only the alleviation of human suffering as a reward for his work, was discouraged and heartbroken at the organized derision. He retired to his home, forgotten by all but his family and his ever-faithful friend, Dr. Chapman, who made the truth known about him wherever and whenever he could.

Ironically, Dr. Gorrie himself was stricken by a fever when he was just fifty-two years old, and he died on June 29, 1853.

Five years later, a Parisian friend of Rosan's, Ferdinand Carré, amid reports that he had profited considerably from hints leaked to him about Dr. Gorrie's work, claimed to be the inventor of the first ice-making machine. The manufacture of ice soon became commonplace.

Chapman continued to keep his friend's name alive until 1897, when ice merchant Samuel Whitehead enlisted fellow members of the Southern Ice Exchange to fund a memorial for Dr. Gorrie. Whitehead proposed that each merchant donate the proceeds from the sale of one ton of ice for a monument to honor the man to whom they owed so much. The grateful members agreed, and the memorial in front of Trinity Church in Apalachicola was dedicated in 1900.

Befitting one of the nineteenth century's great inventors, the original model of Dr. Gorrie's machine is on exhibit in the Smithsonian Institution. In 1914, the doctor's great-granddaughter, Florida senators, Samuel Whitehead, and members of the Southern Ice Exchange were present at the unveiling of a marble likeness of the great inventor and humanitarian in the National Statuary Hall in the Capitol in Washington, DC.

1887

Barefoot Mailmen

In the late nineteenth century, long before the US Postal Service faced anthrax spores or employees "going postal," South Florida mail carriers dealt with wild animals, mail routes that took a week to complete, and a workplace that was literally a jungle.

The distance between Miami and Palm Beach is sixty-eight miles, but in the mid-1800s, a letter sent between those cities would be transported by boat to Key West, Cuba, New York, and Jacksonville before arriving at its destination, some three thousand miles and six to eight weeks later. As the population increased, people demanded more dependable mail delivery, resulting in a service so unique that the carriers became legends. Officially, it was called a "star route," a mail delivery route contracted to a private carrier. But it became better known as the route of the barefoot mailmen—the stuff of postcards, billboards, a novel, a motion picture, and a gift boutique in a Palm Beach mall.

At the time, there were no roads, no railroads, not even a path between Miami and Palm Beach. So desolate was the area that in 1875 the US Life Saving Service began building five Houses of Refuge at intervals along the coast for shipwrecked sailors who otherwise had little chance of survival, unless they could, against all odds, signal a passing steamer. Short of hacking through the jungle with a machete, the beach was the only way across the land. Thus, the mail carriers took to the sand.

Barefoot mailmen, fifteen in all, were necessarily young, strong, brave, and healthy. They had to be, to cover 136 miles round-trip in six days, rest one day, then start all over again the following day—all in the searing Florida sun, confronting torrential rains or hurricanes, and facing mosquitoes and wild animals. The salary for walking over seven thousand miles a year was six hundred dollars annually, but less if men were late or absent, which happened just two times.

The first incident of tardiness occurred in 1886, when the few settlers along the route awakened to find their beach covered with hundreds of casks of wine—Spanish claret, according to the labels. It was said that in one area, casks were so close together along the beach that one could have walked a mile without stepping in sand. More than fifty miles of beach, from Biscayne Bay to the Indian River, were strewn with casks of claret, interspersed with fifteen-gallon kegs of Malaga and Double Superior, all bearing Spanish labels. Strangely, no other wreckage ever appeared, nor did settlers hear of any wreck along the coast. Within a week, all the casks disappeared, some washed out to sea, others confiscated by settlers in what became known as the "Great Wine Wreck." Reasons for the late mail delivery that week were suspect, but the settlers were blissfully unconcerned.

The barefoot mailmen's usual routine was as follows:

Monday: Pick up mail in Palm Beach. Sail down Lake Worth to Boynton Inlet. Walk five miles across Boynton Beach. Rest the first night at Orange Grove House of Refuge in Delray Beach.

Tuesday: Walk seven miles to Hillsborough Inlet. Cross the inlet in a small government boat kept hidden in the bushes for that purpose. Walk eighteen miles to Fort Lauderdale and spend the second night at the New River House of Refuge.

Wednesday: Row four miles down New River to the inlet. Walk ten miles to the top of Biscayne Bay. Sail if the wind was favorable; row if it was not. Reach Miami Wednesday night.

Thursday: Begin return trip in the morning.

The men would return to Palm Beach late Saturday night, having traveled approximately eighty miles on foot and fifty-six by boat. They would rest on Sunday and start over again on Monday morning. To prevent fatigue, the mailmen developed a peculiar, barefoot walk on the hard-packed, slanting sand at the water's edge. Heading south, the right foot moved a bit quicker than the left. Heading north, the left moved more quickly.

They tied their shoes together and slung them over their shoulders along with their mail sack and a haversack. The US Postal Service permitted barefoot mailmen to carry lightweight canvas mail sacks rather than the standard cowhide ones used in the rest of the country. The haversack held hard biscuits, salt pork, coffee, a small frying pan, a tin cup, and matches. The mailmen fortified their scanty diet with fish from the ocean, oysters found near roots in the water, and wild oranges and bananas. Occasional turtle eggs were a special treat, and sea grape leaves made fine dishes. Caves supplied shelter from sudden storms, and drinking water was collected in barrels scattered along the way.

While the barefoot mailmen sometimes experienced harrowing encounters with alligators, panthers, venomous snakes, wild boars, and bears, not to mention swarms of mosquitoes and sand flies, they also were the exclusive audience for exuberant dolphins and fish jumping from the water, sandpipers playing at the water's edge, the amazing straight-down dives of pelicans, and blue herons meditating. They discovered treasure troves of sand dollars and other perfect shells seemingly reserved for them alone.

The fall of 1887 was an unusually stormy one, with torrential rains and swollen rivers, but on Sunday, October 9, the skies cleared to a brilliant blue and the winds died. At dinner with friends, James E. "Ed" Hamilton, a thirty-three-year-old barefoot mailman formerly of Trigg County, Kentucky, mentioned not feeling quite in the pink. Someone suggested he might delay starting his route on Monday morning, but Ed, joking about the "medicine chest" he carried with him—a bottle of Perry-Davis Pain Killer and a spoon—was determined to carry out his duties.

The next day, shouldering his sacks, he headed south toward the Orange Grove House of Refuge. He was never seen again.

When Ed was late arriving back on his return route, friends at first were unconcerned. Since he had been feeling poorly when he left, they assumed he had probably rested for a time and would return the following day. Soon, however, the keeper from the Fort Lauderdale House of Refuge arrived with the news that Ed had never reached his place going south. The keeper also recalled a stranger walking south on the Fort Lauderdale beach the previous Monday. He was suspicious of the man's tale about crossing the river with a hunting party, believing that the stranger had used the mailmen's boat to cross to the south side of the river. A search retracing Ed's path began. In a chilling discovery, Ed's clothes, mail sack, and haversack were found dangling from the limb of a sea grape tree near the spot where his boat should have been. His underclothes lay near the water.

The inescapable conclusion was that when Ed found his boat missing, he stripped, started swimming across the two-hundred-foot channel, and drowned.

Some friends were not so sure. For one thing, Ed was young, over six feet tall, a strong swimmer, and resourceful on land or water. Also disturbing was the large number of alligator tracks in the area. Freshwater from the Everglades had swollen the inlet, which still teemed with the creatures.

The grim scenario seemed confirmed a few years later when a hunting party in the area found a jawbone containing a gold-filled tooth believed to have been Ed's. Ed's friends, reluctantly, sadly concluded that he had been devoured by alligators.

Barefoot mailmen continued operating until a crude road was completed from just below Palm Beach to Miami in 1893, allowing mail to be moved over land. In 1937, near the suspected scene of Ed's demise, the Lake Worth Pioneer Association installed a bronze plaque in honor of James E. Hamilton beneath the Hillsboro Lighthouse.

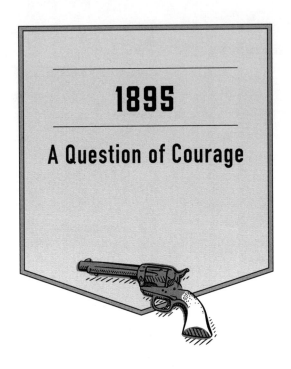

1895

A Question of Courage

Women were not welcome in the practice of medicine in the 1800s, either by physicians or by most of the public. It took a special kind of woman to be willing to endure the hardships, contempt, and accusations of immorality that went along with her medical education and life thereafter. Nevertheless, some women who felt called to the medical profession persisted in pursuing the career and eventually, in answer to their needs, the Woman's Medical College of Philadelphia opened in 1850. That institution fulfilled the need for classroom instruction, but it was still difficult for women to get bedside instruction—experience caring for real, living patients. Finally, in 1869, an affiliation was arranged for female medical students to monitor clinics at Pennsylvania Hospital. They couldn't touch the patients, but they could watch.

On November 6, 1869, when thirty female students entered the amphitheater to observe hospital doctors in action, they were greeted by several hundred male students from all of Philadelphia's medical schools—with hoots, sneers, and ridicule. At the end of the session, as the women were leaving, the male students quickly formed two lines, a gauntlet, forcing the young women to pass between them while the men hurled insults and foul language. Following the females outside, the gentlemen's assault continued, accompanied by a barrage of objects that included tobacco quids and juice.

On March 13, 1879—a scant ten years later—Eleanor Galt recalled the stories of those events when she proudly received her degree, doctor of medicine, at the twenty-seventh annual commencement held at the Women's Medical College's Association Hall. Subsequent to graduation, Galt would pursue a medical career with the same courage and tenacity those women had possessed.

After practicing her profession for a time in New York and New Jersey hospitals, the petite, blonde doctor married a lawyer, Albion R. Simmons, in 1891 and moved to Coconut Grove, Florida. Using plans from *Encyclopedia Britannica,* the couple built a house and also a rock structure that Dr. Simmons used as an office, which still stands. Her husband became interested in making guava jelly and wine, eventually building a factory and shipping his products as far away as London.

As Dade County's first woman physician, Dr. Simmons's strength of character would be severely tested under the conditions of what was then a rough frontier. She made her rounds by horse or mule with a two-wheeled cart, encountering not only alligators and swarms of mosquitoes but also rattlesnakes and an occasional panther. When the Spanish–American War brought seventy-five hundred troops to Miami in 1898, poor sanitation in the camps led to contaminated water supplies, with accompanying typhoid, measles, and dysentery. One soldier wrote to his folks: "If I owned both Miami and Hell, I'd get rid of Miami and live in Hell." Dr. Simmons made visits to the camps and donated badly needed mosquito nets to the hospital to cover the beds.

Even with all the challenges she faced, Dr. Simmons could hardly have expected to be involved with a notorious saloonkeeper or a shootout or any of the rest of the mayhem that occurred in the summer of 1895.

The saloonkeeper in question was the handsome S. S. Lewis. His first name was Sam, but his initials were also said to stand for "Sure Shot." He was a famous marksman, the owner of a rifle he lovingly called Nancy, and he included guitar playing and dancing among his talents. On the night of July 26, 1895, a drunken fight erupted in the Lewis saloon and poolroom. Although there are many versions of the story, most accounts agree that Sure Shot, in attempting to break up the fight, was thwarted when he reached for his gun and someone knifed him. When the night ended, the only other thing agreed upon was that the affair was not over. There would be more trouble for certain.

Lewis lost no time when he spotted the two troublemakers in the street the next morning. Grabbing Nancy, he confronted them, demanding an apology. When none was forthcoming, he summarily shot both men dead. The entire town was stunned almost into paralysis. The bodies lay where they had fallen. In the confusion, Sure Shot Lewis evaded a posse and disappeared.

After a short stay in Bimini, during which almost every Lemon City citizen reported spotting him at one time or another, Lewis made the mistake of returning to Miami on a tiny sailboat. Two members of the posse, with orders to shoot him on sight, had been guarding bay-front property when they spotted him coming ashore. One of the men fired, badly wounding Lewis, who nonetheless managed to return fire. Lewis killed one man and wounded the other before crawling to a shed on the property. Other posse members soon arrived and borrowed Miami founder Julia Tuttle's boat to go to Coconut Grove and bring Dr. Eleanor Simmons back to treat the wounded posse man.

It was three o'clock in the morning when the one-hundred-pound doctor, in a long skirt and high-button shoes, arrived. Swiftly, she tended to Lewis's victim, who was in great pain and had lost much blood from one neck wound and two bullet holes in his side. She made him as comfortable as she could under the circumstances and then informed the posse, "Men, I am going to the wounded man to do my duty as a doctor. Please do him no harm while I am in there."

The men of the posse watched silently as Dr. Simmons strode to the shack, calling through the door, "Mr. Lewis, this is Dr. Simmons. Can I do anything for you?"

"Yes," came the weak voice from inside. "I am all shot up. Come in quick. If anyone comes with you, I will kill him."

Carrying her medical bag and a lantern, Dr. Simmons shoved the door open and disappeared, leaving the nervous posse behind. By the light of her lantern, she removed two bullets from Sure Shot's right thigh and one from his left leg. After dressing the wounds, she splinted the compound fracture of his left leg as best she could.

Her patient informed her that he fully expected to be lynched and begged her to supply him with enough chloroform so he might put himself to sleep—permanently. She refused, of course, and a few hours later, miserable with pain and thirst, Sure Shot allowed a friend to remove his guns from the shack before he surrendered.

The Lady Doctor from Coconut Grove would have been amused if she had heard one male colleague's recorded opinion of women's ability to practice medicine, expounded as late as 1900: "The whole question of women's place in medicine hinges on the fact that, when a critical case demands independent action and fearless judgment, man's success depends on his virile courage, which the normal woman does not have nor is expected to have." Little did he know, Dr. Simmons and countless other women doctors had already proved him terribly wrong.

1901

Henry Flagler's Divorce

Henry Flagler was the benevolent father of Florida's east coast. He opened up the Florida jungle by running his railroad the length of it, creating the cities of Palm Beach, West Palm Beach, and Miami. He ruled them with an iron hand, although he was never elected to any office. His money built churches, a hospital, and schools, and installed water and electricity in the settlements. He founded newspapers and refused to stamp his name anywhere on Florida. When the big freezes of 1894–1895 and 1896–1897 wiped out citrus crops, Flagler lost no time helping growers recover.

He was a man who aroused envy, respect, gratitude, and admiration, but all that changed in 1901, when he was denounced from pulpits, excoriated in newspapers, and blamed for several legislators' being defeated at the polls.

The railroad tycoon was accused of "buying" the legislature in order to push through a law he needed to divorce his insane wife and marry another woman. Although time eventually faded some of the bitterness, his tarnished reputation never quite regained its luster.

The eighth-grade dropout had already made a name for himself before he arrived in Florida. Born in New York, Henry Flagler migrated to Cleveland, Ohio, where he joined forces with John D. Rockefeller to form the greatest industrial empire of the age, the Standard Oil Company. Although Flagler was content to allow Rockefeller's name to outshine his own, he was credited by Rockefeller himself as being the brains of the firm, the one with the most imagination.

Flagler married a lovely but frail young woman, Mary Harkness, whose health continued to fade as the fortunes of Standard Oil increased. In the winter of 1876, while the Flaglers were living in New York, doctors advised traveling to the warm sunshine and salt air of Florida in hopes of healing Mary.

At the time, Florida's population of 250,000 was settled mainly along the northern border. Except for Key West, the largest city at ten thousand people, the rest of Florida was mostly unsettled territory. Reluctantly, the scion of Standard Oil took his family to this wilderness and, in short order, reported that St. Augustine was "a pesthole," Jacksonville was "awful," there was nothing to do, and he was bored. A few weeks later, he returned to New York with his wife and family. It was against doctors' orders, but Mary refused to stay in Florida without him and Henry Flagler would not stay.

Back in New York, as expected, Mary's health continued to deteriorate, requiring Henry to hire his wife a full-time companion, a former actress named Ida Alice Shourds.

Although his refusal to remain with Mary in a more healthful climate seems heartless, Henry Flagler never spent more than two nights away from home in their seventeen-year marriage. He preferred to spend evenings reading to his wife until her death in 1881, at which time he openly dated Ida Alice. Two years later, they were married.

By that time, his business know-how was no longer critical to Standard Oil, and Henry Flagler craved new challenges. Land deals in Florida were becoming more and more attractive, leading him to his second full-fledged career in 1885. On a return visit to the state, he revised his original opinion, recognizing some exciting possibilities. "I believe," he said, "we can make St. Augustine the Newport of the South."

The Newport of the North was a vacation area for wealthy Americans. To pattern St. Augustine after it would require, among other things, first-class hotels. As it happened, during his stay St. Augustine was commemorating the landing of Ponce de León, a celebration that made such an impression on Henry Flagler that he began planning his first Florida hotel, the Ponce de León, which upon completion would become the largest concrete structure in the world. Although never one to spend money foolishly, he spared no expense to make his hotel the best in the world, complete with a breathtaking three-story rotunda in the lobby.

Ida Alice enthusiastically threw herself into the budding social scene, enjoying her newfound position and ability to spend money in quantities she never could have imagined. She indulged in vicious gossip and threw frequent temper tantrums, interrupting parties and balls. Flagler, however, found her charming—until her Ouija board told her the czar of Russia was in love with her and planned to marry her upon Flagler's death. When she paid two thousand dollars to Tiffany's to have her miniature painted, surrounded with diamonds, then sent to the czar (whom she had never met), it got Flagler's attention. He canceled the order and had her seen by a psychiatrist friend. As president of the Lunacy Commission of New York, the doctor was empowered to commit her to an asylum. Reluctant at first, he changed his mind, diagnosing her "incurably insane" after she injured him with scissors she had hidden.

Sometime during this turmoil, Flagler, seventy-one years old and understandably depressed, began to be seen in the company of his cousin, Eliza Ashley, along with her friend, an accomplished musician, thirty-four-year-old Mary Lily Kenan. The younger women, especially Mary Lily, helped lift Flagler from his depression. Soon, he was openly escorting Mary Lily to social functions, as aristocratic tongues wagged.

Seemingly reenergized and not content with developing his resort in St. Augustine, Flagler began planning resorts all along Florida's eastern seaboard. To service his resorts, he bought or built railroads, forming the Florida East Coast Railway, creating jobs and sparking reciprocal loyalty between him and his employees. Before long, passengers could board a train in New York City and ride all the way to Daytona. After creating Palm Beach for wealthy vacationers, it was necessary to build West Palm Beach to house workers for the resort. Next, Miami was developed, all thanks to Henry Flagler.

In the meantime, however, as gossips had a field day, Mary Lily and her family pressed Flagler concerning his intentions. He bought some time by building Mary Lily a Palm Beach home and giving her one million dollars in Standard Oil stock plus some pearl baubles worth another million. After that, he started the wheels of entitlement turning.

His plan was simple. Sole grounds for divorce in New York, where he was a legal resident, and in Florida were adultery. He first changed his residence to Florida, for "business reasons." Next, he petitioned the New York courts to declare Ida Alice insane; he succeeded. Finally, he had accommodating friends introduce a bill in the Florida legislature making insanity grounds for divorce. It took just two weeks from the time the bill was submitted until its signing by Governor William S. Jennings. Ten days after the bill became law, Mary Lily became the third Mrs. Henry Flagler.

Reaction was swift. Florida's conservative morality was outraged. With the exception of the Ocala *Banner*, newspapers in the state outdid one another with scathing editorials. Seventy years later, Florida East Coast Railway files revealed the truth—Flagler had made $125,000 worth of payoffs.

Some politicians who voted for the bill lost elections because of their votes. The Flaglers, ignoring gossip, editorials, and attacks from the pulpit, lived their lives much as before for the next twelve years until Henry's death, followed by Mary Lily's four years later. Ida Alice, meanwhile, having been provided for generously by her ex-husband, lived in the New York sanitarium, obliviously consulting her Ouija board, and planning her wedding to the czar. Her estate was valued at fifteen million dollars when she died at age eighty-two.

1908

Tampa Nurse Builds a Hospital

The year was 1908, a time when both Black and White Floridians were dying for lack of hospital care. In addition, the only public hospital in Tampa did not admit African American patients.

Dr. M. R. Winton, a prominent, caring White physician, found himself grappling with a familiar dilemma. A patient in his care, a good, hard-working woman, had a tumor that needed to be operated on, and there was no time to waste. But she was Black. No local hospital would admit her, and even he could not change the rules.

There was nothing to be done but make the patient as comfortable as possible in her home and try to ease her pain. Accordingly, Dr. Winton enlisted the help of Clara Frye, a nurse who worked for several eminent physicians in the city and who had the reputation for being "the best fever nurse" in Tampa. Clara did what she could for the patient but, knowing her care was inadequate and that surgery was needed, she suggested to Dr. Winton that they might improvise an operating room in a cottage she knew of in Tampa Heights. He readily agreed.

The three-room cottage at 1615 Lamar Avenue, shaded by trees and surrounded by a picket fence, was Clara's own home. At Dr. Winton's instructions, equipment was brought in and the room was prepared. The patient was moved to the cottage and readied for surgery. It was simply impossible to have an operating table moved into the tiny cottage, but Dr. Winton and the ever-resourceful nurse didn't let that stop them. The dining room table filled in nicely, and the tumor was removed successfully. The patient remained at the cottage while she recovered uneventfully, unaware that the bed she occupied was Clara's own. The nurse, in the meantime, slept on a pallet on the floor.

In a short time, three more patients came to the cottage for treatment. Clara, seeing evidence of a real need, decided to remain "in charge of the little cottage and make it a part of my lifework." It seemed a fitting undertaking for a woman who had dreamed of being a nurse ever since her childhood.

The fair-skinned Clara was born in New York in 1872, the daughter of a White English mother and a Black Southern father. Her family moved to Montgomery, Alabama, when Clara was ten years old. When she was old enough, she traveled to Chicago, where she studied nursing for two years. After practicing nursing for the next sixteen years in Montgomery, she relocated to Tampa, Florida, in 1901 and married a Tampa barber named Sherman Frye. Intelligent, reliable, and compassionate, she soon enjoyed an excellent professional reputation. While working for several eminent doctors, she also nursed the children of Tampa's mayor, D. B. McKay. One of those children, Aurora McKay, was quoted as saying, "She was a wonderful person. When we needed care, she would give it. When we needed a spanking, she gave us that, too."

But it was with the conversion of her cottage to a hospital that Clara made her greatest contribution. In the beginning, she had only a few beds and the facilities were primitive. Her friend and colleague, Mary T. Cash, also a nurse, was Clara's valued right hand. She later recalled that early on, all the surgical instruments had to be sterilized in a washtub in the backyard. Although the city contributed some money for charity patients, it was far from enough. The few paying patients were not in a position to pay very much, so finances were always a problem. In 1916, Clara and seven other nurses solicited passersby in the downtown city streets on a "tag day," netting them $221, which seemed like a fortune. Mayor McKay once described Clara as "the good woman who gave the Negroes of Tampa their first hospital and whose kind heart kept her constantly in financial difficulties."

There were countless times when she could not pay her own bills, but somehow by 1923, with the help of a thousand-dollar loan from Dr. Winton, Clara managed to purchase a two-story building on Lamar Street. With the added space, she was able to care for more Black charity patients, many referred to her by Dr. J. P. Lawrence, the city physician, although she worked without any official contract. Ella Chamberlain, a Tampa suffragist, was instrumental in sending many patients to Clara, some from prisons, some from the slums, all in need. Some groups donated cash and useful goods, and it was all gratefully accepted.

"Here we are today in a real building with almost every convenience," Clara said enthusiastically. Then she quietly added, "But at what personal sacrifice nobody knows. There were nights when my pillow was wet with tears and my eyes burned for just one minute of restful sleep."

Charity patients usually filled the entire seventeen-bed ward on the first floor, while the twenty-nine beds on the second floor were occupied by private patients. According to a 1925 report on African American life in Tampa, the frame building was a fire hazard, there was a persistent lack of drugs, and there were other inadequacies. It was carefully noted that Clara herself was not to be blamed.

The report must have been particularly bitter medicine, since in 1925 voters had passed a bond issue for construction of a new hospital, but none of the money was designated for African American care. According to nurse Mary Cash, Clara never turned anyone away, whatever their color or circumstance.

In 1930 and 1931, the City of Tampa bought Clara's hospital, renaming it the Municipal Hospital for Negroes. Dr. J. A. White, Tampa's first African American surgeon, was named the hospital medical director. But hard times would continue for the institution due to inadequate funding and the national financial disaster known as the Great Depression.

All the same, the sale allowed Clara to move into a home of her own, but according to Mary Cash, even then Clara remained poor and humble because "she never turned anybody away for a meal."

Sixty-three-year-old Clara Frye died in poverty at her home at 3303 34th Street on April 8, 1936, and was buried in the family plot in Woodlawn Cemetery. Years later, her old friend, Dr. Winton, stated, "If I went to Heaven today, I expect the first person I'd meet would be Clara Frye."

1911

A Chinese Man's Faith in America

In 1911, the American Pomological Society, the oldest organization in North America devoted to fruit growing, provided a pleasant interruption to Floridian Lue Gim Gong's lonely existence. The orange he had developed won the Wilder Silver Medal, their highest award. Even the US Department of Agriculture pronounced Lue's orange special. It made the years of being an outsider, of loneliness and hard work, seem worthwhile. Unfortunately, at the same time, his burgeoning reputation was also attracting unscrupulous growers trying to capitalize on his fame and impose on his good nature.

The elderly man in tattered clothes was a long-standing victim of tuberculosis. His vision was fading, and his savings were gone when he received the cruelest blow of all—he would lose his DeLand, Florida, home and citrus groves unless he could pay the interest on money he had borrowed. Lue Gim Gong had no chance of coming up with the money.

As a boy in Canton, China, Lue had helped plow, plant, harvest, and market vegetables from the family fields and citrus from their groves in the subtropical "rice bowl of China." He had learned from his mother how to transfer pollen from the flower of one plant to the flower of another one possessing different qualities, resulting in a third plant with the qualities of the first two. It was this delicate skill that would one day earn him great rewards.

When an uncle who had lived in San Francisco's Chinatown told Lue how there were so many schools in the United States that even girls were permitted to attend, Lue knew he had to find a way to reach that land of opportunity.

After his uncle bought his ticket and arranged for him to stay with a friend in San Francisco, Lue's parents reluctantly gave their permission. The shy twelve-year-old spent two lonely, agonizing months on a small cargo ship, tossed about on the ocean, with bad, insufficient food, and after it was over, he could never bear to think of it again.

He was lucky to find work in a shoe factory. Many of his countrymen were indentured, owing years of wages to agents who had arranged their passage. It was not a good time to be Chinese in America. The first Chinese migrants, brought to the United States twenty years earlier to help in the gold rush, stayed to complete the transcontinental railroad. When the railroad was finished in 1869, many of these six thousand men were unemployed and starving. Out-of-work White Americans blamed the easily identified Chinese for taking jobs away. Some Chinese were beaten or stoned, and the only work many could find was in laundries or restaurants or as houseboys. The Exclusion Act was passed in 1882, making the Chinese the only nationality ever barred from immigration in US history.

The owner of the shoe factory where Lue worked also owned a factory in Massachusetts, where he had previously broken a strike by hiring unemployed Chinese men from San Francisco. He was so impressed with the work of the first group that he sent for another fifty Chinese men. Lue was among them.

As the immigrants tried to adapt to the cold climate and the new language, local ministers organized a Sunday school for them. Disregarding the fact that China had a civilization one thousand years before the Greeks built the Parthenon, the ministers considered the Chinese to be heathens who needed to be Christianized. Townspeople wanting to help often invited the Chinese into their homes. In this way, Lue met Frances Burlingame, a teacher who was much impressed with Lue's intelligence during one of his visits. She gave him extra lessons, then invited him to stay in the Burlingame home, where in exchange for helping in the gardens, she would try to satisfy his intense thirst for education.

For the first time in his life, Lue had his own room and more books than he could ever hope to read, and he was encouraged to learn as much as he could. Before long, teacher and pupil were more like mother and son, and he was addressing her as "Mother Fannie."

Tolerated by some wealthy Burlingame acquaintances, scorned by others, Lue considered himself blessed. He missed his Chinese family, but he disgraced them by refusing to marry the Chinese bride they had chosen for him. He had become very Americanized and was subsequently disowned by his family. When Mother Fannie moved to DeLand,

Florida, where the family had purchased citrus groves, Lue went with her. Within a year, Lue Gim Gong was a proud American citizen.

For the next few years, he managed the groves for Fannie and her widowed sister while he conducted experiments with fruit. Remembering those precious lessons from his Chinese mother, he combined the best qualities of two different oranges to create the Lue Gim Gong orange, which was sweet, hardy, and able to withstand sudden cold snaps. The juicy orange was also sturdy enough to adhere to the tree through the summer rains, and it sold for a good price. Able to stay fresh for a long period, Lue Gim Gong oranges shipped well, making them highly competitive with California oranges.

Lue became known as "the Chinese Burbank," after Luther Burbank, a famous horticulturist. Among the unusual plant combinations Lue produced were a rosebush with seventeen varieties of roses in seven colors from a single root. A grapefruit he created that was twenty-one inches in circumference was too pithy for eating, but it made a delightful room freshener and its skin was perfect for candy or pickling.

With Mother Fannie's death in 1903, Lue lost his shield against the cruel intolerance of strangers, acquaintances, and even some Burlingame family members. That was when nurseries tricked him into making misleading agreements and illegally sold his stock to unprincipled growers. Those contracts with nurseries cost the trusting Lue a great deal of money and led him into the dire financial straits that threatened the Florida home and groves willed to him by Mother Fannie. Fortunately, Edgar Wright, who had known and admired Lue for a long time, intervened. Wright, editor of a horticultural magazine, the *Florida Grower,* appealed to readers for help.

"Nobody can know him without loving him," he said of Lue. "Let us give this meek and lowly man a square deal." Contributions were so generous that Lue was secure until his death in 1925. His faith in his adopted homeland was validated. In his will, Lue thanked the Lord for allowing him to live "in this great good country of ours."

Lue would surely have smiled when the orange, which originated in China thousands of years ago and advanced through his humble contributions, came full circle in the year 2000, when China finally agreed to open its markets to Florida citrus.

1921

Carl and His Elephant

If some people seem to thrive on action, speed, and upheaval of any kind, Carl Fisher would have to be their role model. From his Indiana childhood when he did headstands on fences and walked on stilts so high they had to be mounted from the second story of his mother's house, Carl's daredevil instinct was strong.

Machines, races, and excitement figured large in Fisher's life when he and his wife, Jane, first vacationed in Miami in 1910. During an inspection tour of some new property, Jane slapped at huge flies and mosquitoes and shuddered at an alligator roaring nearby, but her husband nearly exploded with glee.

"Look, honey, I'm going to build a city here!" he said. "A city like magic, like romantic places you read about and dream about, but never see. It's going to be a place where the old can grow young, and the young never grow old—the sort of place Ponce de León dreamed about."

An older man, John Collins, had run out of money trying to build a bridge to the spit of overgrown land across the bay from Miami. In return for a fifty-thousand-dollar loan, Collins deeded two hundred acres of his land to Carl, and with another two hundred acres he bought, Fisher was launched on yet another adventure and another challenge to his ingenuity at generating publicity.

Young Carl knew lean times after his father disappeared, leaving his mother, Ida, to open a boardinghouse in Indianapolis to provide for her three boys. Deciding he'd had enough of school, daredevil Carl left a study hall in sixth grade and began his working life sweeping a grocery store and hawking newspapers on trains. By the time he was seventeen, he'd saved enough to open a bicycle repair shop, just as the great bicycle craze was sweeping the nation.

Before long, Carl was able to sell bicycles, then motorcycles, then automobiles, and his talent for whipping up promotions became legendary. He and his brothers built the "largest bike in the world," a twenty-foot-high contraption that drew crowds so large police had to intervene. Carl followed that escapade with a highly publicized bicycle ride on a tightrope stretched between two twelve-story buildings.

As Fisher's interest migrated from bikes to autos, his flamboyant stunts grew more ambitious, and his circle of cronies expanded to include anyone who was anyone in the fledgling world of the automobile. With two partners, he founded the Prest-O-Lite corporation, which manufactured headlights for cars and which earned the partners nine million dollars when they sold it in 1913.

But concentrating on one thing at a time was not in Carl Fisher's makeup. In 1909, thirty-four-year-old Carl married fifteen-year-old Jane Watts and built "the greatest race track in the world," the Indianapolis Motor Speedway. He rode the pace car in the first Memorial Day Indy 500.

Taking advantage of his contacts in the automobile business, Fisher was a major player in bringing the nation's first transcontinental road, the Lincoln Highway, into existence. He then pressured the same associates and promoted the north-south Dixie Highway.

All this was a prelude to his and Jane's first trip to Miami, where he was attracted to the climate and lifestyle and also recognized a promising opportunity when he saw one. Shortly after Fisher's business dealings with John Collins, the dirt began to fly. Older Miami residents shook their heads in amazement at the "damned fool" who "pumped tons of sand into a swamp" to create an island called Miami Beach. As he dredged and developed and sold lots, Carl worked to attract his rich friends in the automobile business by building a swimming casino, tennis courts, golf courses, and polo fields. When his friend Julius Fleischmann, of yeast company fame, dropped dead after one of his polo matches, Carl, never one to miss an opportunity for publicity, made sure the story was reported under a Miami Beach dateline.

Carl organized and publicized sailing regattas, deep-sea fishing trips, and speedboat races. When people, including local ministers, were shocked by Jane's abbreviated swimming apparel (no stockings and a skirt that came just to her knees), Carl was elated. Pictures of good-looking, burnished young people in bathing suits soon flooded the country, advertising Miami Beach.

With the Florida boom of the 1920s, Carl was not the only developer seeking buyers. Competition arose in Coral Gables and Boca Raton. Always on the lookout for a gimmick, he made good use of an elephant named Rosie presented to him by a friend who was the former owner of a circus. An elephant is hard to ignore under any circumstances, and Carl managed to have Rosie present for every wire service photo opportunity imaginable—pulling kiddie carts, attending grand openings, whatever. Still, sales lagged behind his expectations.

In the winter of 1920, word circulated on the grapevine that newly elected President Warren G. Harding was planning a Florida visit. Carl plunged into a spirited campaign to entice the president to Miami Beach—specifically to Fisher's Flamingo Hotel, scheduled to open in three weeks. The publicity resulting from a US president's stay would ensure a full house for months, even years to come. Carl started the ball rolling with an offer to the president of a free suite of rooms, promising privacy, luxury, and relaxation, and guaranteeing sunny skies for golf, deep-sea fishing, or whatever diversion was desired. He enlisted state senators he was acquainted with to put in a good word when they could—any influence he could use, he did.

Needless to say, the competition was not sitting still. For several months, developers in the Miami area made offers and waited. It looked promising. Then it didn't. Finally, when Carl's natural, good-natured optimism was deserting him, he made one last attempt, sending one of his very attractive female assistants to make a personal pitch to President Harding. Warren G. Harding was known to be a connoisseur of feminine beauty, and he reached a decision. He and his wife vacationed at the Flamingo Hotel. From the moment of the president's arrival in South Florida, Carl Fisher seldom left his side.

Flash bulbs popped, stories with a Miami Beach dateline flooded the wires, and Harding's enthusiastic public endorsement of Miami Beach was a publicity man's dream come true. One batch of photos showed the genial president on the golf course with his caddy, Rosie the elephant. Sales of Miami Beach property soared until the legendary hurricane of 1926 ended the Florida boom for everyone, including Carl Fisher.

1922

Marjory's Poem

She would become a world-famous environmentalist before the term became popular, a feminist before that word was invented, and a civil rights activist before much of the world was conscious of such things. But in 1922 Marjory Stoneman Douglas was simply a young assistant editor and daily columnist for the *Miami Herald,* a newspaper owned by her father.

In her role as a journalist, she met many people, some famous, some seeking her out to publicize their pet projects. She was privy to stories before they went into print and to some that never did. She considered herself sophisticated and professional, but the story of the arrest and subsequent death of a young man trapped in Florida's brutal convict-lease system was nearly more than Marjory could bear.

Of course, she had been aware of the existence of the convict-lease system in Florida, but she'd had no reason to delve deeply into that unpleasantness, which had existed for fifty years. Crimes and punishment had gone on for a long time.

In 1570, Spanish soldiers built a prison in St. Augustine, the first in the New World outside of Mexico. From that point on, interest in the construction of a prison system faded from Florida's consciousness, as it did from most southern states, partly because plantation owners administered punishments in private and the law never needed to be involved.

When the Civil War ended, most of the South, including Florida, was destitute, and crime among both White and Black people was increasing. With no money to build prisons, impoverished states began leasing out groups of prisoners to private concerns such as lumber camps, turpentine camps, phosphate mines, road and railroad contractors, and farm and plantation owners. The lessee was responsible for the convicts' food, clothing, housing, and medical care, although the latter was generally nonexistent. Nevertheless, it was a money-making scheme for the states. It was also a half century of relentless brutality.

Improperly clothed prisoners were worked from dawn to dusk, then chained to their beds at night. Fed inadequately, many passed out from exhaustion. For the slightest offense, prisoners were forced on runs by guards with bayonets attached to their muskets. Minor infractions were punished by beating prisoners with leather paddles or hanging them by their thumbs with their feet just off the ground until their thumbs became elongated. "Watering," another favorite punishment, consisted of pouring water through a funnel into the mouth until the prisoner suffered unspeakable agony and sometimes died. Solitary confinement was accomplished by means of seven-by-seven-foot "sweat-boxes," which became "ice-boxes" in winter.

At one Jacksonville prison, three women prisoners were harnessed to a plow while other women were forced to guide the plow to cultivate fields. Women were at the mercy of guards, other prisoners, or whatever males happened by.

Florida's convict-lease system was legalized in 1877, and although all other southern states had cruel versions of it, Florida's came to be known as the most inhumane. In a book written by a prison guard named J. C. Powell, Florida's system was called the American Siberia. But it wasn't until a tragic occurrence made news enough to capture the attention of a *Miami Herald* reporter that the rest of the country was forced to confront the ugly practice.

In December 1921, twenty-two-year-old Martin Tabert, a young man from North Dakota, set out on an adventure. He had worked hard on the family farm, saved some money, and, like his older sisters and brothers, Martin wanted to see some of the world. The adventure went well until he ran out of money in Florida. After hopping a freight train in Tallahassee, he was caught and arrested for vagrancy. Unable to pay his fine, he notified his parents, who sent funds in a letter. When the letter was returned to them unopened and stamped, "Unclaimed. Party gone," they assumed their son had found funds somewhere else and had left Tallahassee. They waited to hear from him.

In the meantime, Martin was sentenced to sixty days in a Leon County jail, and then leased to a lumber company in Dixie County. In just two months, by February 1922, the formerly strong young man was reduced to a skeletal, ailing shadow, barely able to drag himself to work. In a delirium and crying for mercy, he was beaten into a coma and died within two days. His parents were informed that he had died of a fever. It would be more than a year before they learned the truth.

Marjory Stoneman Douglas was working late when the wire came from North Florida reporting the tragedy. The vicious snuffing out of the young man's life affected her so deeply that she was unable to concentrate on her work. Pacing back and forth in front of her desk in the half-deserted city room of the *Herald,* she seemed to hear his name over and over in her mind. "Martin Tabert, Martin Tabert." A poem began to form.

By morning, the simple poem was finished, and it headed her column for that day.

> *Martin Tabert of North Dakota is walking Florida now.*
> *O children, hark to his footsteps coming, for he's*
> *walking soft and slow.*
> *Through the piney woods and the cypress hollows,*
> *A wind creeps up and it's him it follows.*
> *Martin Tabert of North Dakota is walking Florida now.*
> *They took him out to the convict camp, and he's*
> *walking Florida now.*
> *O children, the tall pines stood and heard him when*
> *he was moaning low.*
> *The other convicts, they stood around him,*
> *When the length of the black strap cracked and found him.*
> *Martin Tabert of North Dakota. And he's walking*
> *Florida now.*

They nailed his coffin boards together and he's
walking Florida now.
O children, the dark night saw where they buried
him, buried him, buried him low.
And the tall pines heard where they went to hide him.
And the wind crept up to moan beside him.
Martin Tabert of North Dakota. And he's walking
Florida now.
The whip is still in the convict camps, for Florida's
stirring now.
Children, from Key West to Pensacola you can hear
the great wind go.
The wind that he roused when he lay dying,
The angry voice of Florida crying,
Martin Tabert of North Dakota,
Martin Tabert of North Dakota,
Martin Tabert of North Dakota,
You can rest from your walking now.

The poem was highly praised, and the story received enormous attention. The *New York World* published a series of articles on Florida's convict camps that were reprinted throughout the country. Irate editorials ran in Florida papers, generating unfavorable national publicity and jolting civic and religious organizations into action.

Prodded by the North Dakota legislature, the Florida legislature conducted an investigation that resulted in some officials losing their jobs. Marjory's poem was read before the joint legislative meeting, with profound effect.

The man who had beaten Martin Tabert was found guilty of second-degree murder but later acquitted in a new trial. Nonetheless, the march for reform was on, and in 1923, Florida Governor Cary Hardee signed bills abolishing whipping of convicts and the convict-lease system.

Marjory Stoneman Douglas said in her autobiography that she considered these results the single most important thing she accomplished in her writing career.

1923

A Black Town Destroyed

In January 1923, on Florida's west coast, about nine miles from the Gulf of Mexico, the progressive, peaceful, small, mainly Black town of Rosewood was heartlessly destroyed by a large mob of angry White aggressors. Mostly deserted afterward by both White and Black fearful citizens, the sad little town quietly faded away. Until then, Rosewood had been an excellent community where more Black residents owned their own homes and their businesses than almost everywhere else in the entire country.

Originally, Rosewood had been settled by both Black and White people who were chiefly employed in the two pencil factories in nearby Cedar Key. The town was named for the reddish color of the cedar wood used to make pencils in the pencil mills of Cedar Key. Some Rosewood residents also worked in area turpentine mills and others in a nearby sawmill. The town had a train depot and a post office, too, but it was never officially recognized to be a town.

By 1890, most of the cedar trees had been cut down, causing the pencil mills to close and most White residents to move away, settling in the nearby town of Sumner, a chiefly White company town. Only a few White people stayed behind in Rosewood, which resulted in a Black population of about two hundred and one White family who ran a general store.

But by 1920, Rosewood had grown, and its citizens were proud of their three churches, a school, a turpentine mill, a sugarcane mill, and two general stores, one of which was White owned. The town had a baseball team, and everything was managed by a generally contented Black population. A few privileged families even enjoyed having a piano or an organ in their small household.

Although at that time racial violence was common almost everywhere in the nation, the Black residents of Rosewood enjoyed living in their town where they could walk peacefully anywhere they wanted to walk, every day if they wanted to. Knowing how common racial violence was nearly everywhere else made Rosewood even more special to those who lived there.

It was always a fairly peaceful place for the Black residents, but when a poll tax was enacted in 1885, many Black citizens could no longer afford to vote, act as jurors, or run for office, which, of course, aroused feelings of discontent. Understandably, many felt they were not considered first-class citizens.

Racial violence escalated so much in other parts of the country by the summer of 1919 that the people in Rosewood were calling it Red Summer. Sadly, it became known that when an unfortunate Black man tried to vote in a small town not far away, he was stopped in a massive eruption that turned into a massacre.

Florida's election winners satisfied their White voters in many ways. They encouraged Black Floridians to join labor markets in other states, including in the steel industry and on railroads. More than one governor spread the word that there was to be no punishment for lynchings committed in Florida during their terms, and sadly, there were many.

When World War I began, Black troops were trained the same as White troops were, which meant Black soldiers were armed like White ones, a fact that stirred up much alarm among a great number of White citizens when they learned of it. At that time, anti-Black crime had become increasingly frequent. Additionally, German propaganda was deliberately spread to US Black soldiers to promote the idea that their real enemies were the White people in America.

Black troops, though, believed they had joined in the effort to make the whole world safe for democracy, and they believed that they, too, would achieve it and would receive better treatment when they returned to their own country. Unfortunately, when they did return, it didn't take long for them to realize they would not be included in that accomplishment, firming their decision to fight back at home. One result was a huge riot in Houston, Texas, in 1917. It had to be depressing for Black troops to face the reality, but face it they did, and they summoned up a determined will to fight back. They refused to accept their own country's denial of democracy to them.

On January 1, 1923, the screams of a twenty-two-year-old married White woman, Fannie Taylor, caused concerned

Rosewood neighbors to come rushing to investigate, wanting to help her. Visibly shaken, Taylor claimed that a Black man had attacked her in her home and then fled to hide into nearby swamps. Many observant Black neighbors knew this was not the first time a White man visited Fannie Taylor. They believed she and the man were secret lovers who had had a spat and she was probably telling the story of a Black intruder to hide the truth from her husband. He, James Taylor, was totally unaware of his wife's hidden activity, and he intensified the situation by asking for help from White residents in the area, including at a nearby Ku Klux Klan gathering.

County law enforcement, headed by Sheriff Robert Walker, quickly became involved, and upon learning that a Black prisoner, Jesse Hunter, had just escaped from a chain gang and was supposedly still in the area, Walker decided Hunter was most likely the man they were looking for. A search for him began. As it went on, for some unknown reason tracking dogs led another White group to the Rosewood home of Aaron Carrier, whose aunt for some time had been doing all the laundry for Fannie Taylor. Carrier was beaten by the mob, tied to a car, and dragged all the way to Sumner, a nearby mostly White company town, before being released to the sheriff in Bronson, which was the county seat twenty-five miles away.

On January 4, thinking that Hunter was hiding in Sarah Carrier's home, the mob grouped outside her home and fired shots randomly. It became a fierce gun battle involving her son, Sylvester, until eventually Sarah and Sylvester were both killed. The battle lasted all night, and while it had been going on, Black-owned buildings were completely burned to the ground and more Black residents were killed.

Many Black neighbors managed to flee from their homes, staying hidden in the swamps and some in homes of sympathetic White residents who cared for them until they were able to escape from the territory.

Convinced that it was the beginning of a race war, even more White men from the surrounding area stormed into the neighborhood. They attacked houses, churches, and whatever else was Black owned. As they shot any who fled the burning buildings, the Black people who did escape stayed hidden in the swamps for days.

After a few days, the attacking mob began to pull out, except for a few who returned and set fire to what was left of the town, in the process burning every building that had been owned by a Black person. None of the former citizens made any effort to return to the scene of violence, bloodshed, and lives lost, lives that were precious to them. Some even changed their names, hoping to avoid being tracked down by anyone in the future.

The governor appointed a special grand jury to investigate what went on, but after several days of listening to various testimonies, the all-White jury decided there was not nearly enough evidence to prosecute anyone; the jury disbanded.

To this day, no one has ever been prosecuted for the total destruction of the town of Rosewood. There is nothing left of the well-loved town of Rosewood, except for a sign installed where the town did once exist.

At one time, there were hundreds of Black towns in this country, but like Rosewood, most of them are gone.

1928

Saving Betty Mae

On April 27, 1923, Ada Tiger, a full-blooded Seminole member of the Snake clan, was taken by concerned Indian women to a specially prepared birth *chickee* (a palmetto-thatched raised platform, open on all sides) a half-mile away from the Seminole camp at Indiantown. The woman's grandmother, Mary Tiger, delivered a baby girl, Betty Mae. Both mother and child were gently bathed by the women and put to bed, looked after, and fed nourishing meals for four days and four nights before they were returned home, where they remained isolated, except from the women, for four months. All this closely followed the Seminole way, but for one thing: Betty Mae's father, Abe Parton, was White.

Abe, a French sugarcane worker and trapper, lived nearby and was on good terms with the Seminoles, sometimes trading with them. But like any other White man, Abe was considered undesirable as the suitor of an Indian female. As late as the 1920s, young Seminole women who became involved with White men were severely beaten, sometimes to the point of incapacitating them for days, while their lovers, if caught, were killed. All mixed-race babies were thought to be evil and were destroyed by either stuffing their mouths with mud or simply throwing them into the water.

Nursing hard feelings as a result of the three Seminole wars, the men of Indiantown were a particularly unyielding group. Being directly descended from the war band of Billy Bowlegs surely added to their bitter attitude. Billy, who was credited with having started the Third Seminole War single-handedly, would never knowingly collaborate with any White men.

Betty Mae and her family managed to endure the discrimination coming from all sides until she was about five years old and her baby brother, Howard, was nearly two. That was when, late one night, a crowd of Indiantown men appeared with guns, shouting and demanding that the children be killed before they brought bad luck upon the tribe.

They failed to reckon with Great-Uncle Jimmie Gopher, who had been expecting them from the day Betty Mae was born. He was a powerful man in the tribe, a highly respected medicine man. He and Grandpa Tom Tiger were prepared with rifles loaded to safeguard the lives of the children. Shouts grew louder and anger escalated until Great-Uncle Jimmie shot into the crowd, hitting some of the bloodthirsty men as they fled. The children's lives were saved, but Great-Uncle Jimmie was taken to jail. The arresting marshal respectfully waited before taking him away, giving Jimmie time to issue a warning in Seminole to bystanders that if the children were harmed during his absence, he would seek revenge upon his return.

Even though the children were spared, the family was no longer comfortable in Indiantown, and when Jimmie Gopher was released from jail, they moved with other Seminoles to Dania village, later the site of the Hollywood Seminole Indian reservation.

The children's father disappeared, heading west, and life was very hard for the family. Mother and grandmother both worked in the fields, picking beans and tomatoes. Great-Uncle Jimmie found some work on the reservation, and the children did what they could to help the poor-but-close family group.

Influenced by an older girl who read books, Betty Mae became consumed with a desire to learn to read. Neither the school for Black children nor the one for White children would accept her, but Great-Uncle Jimmie came through again. Through contact with the Indian agent, he secured a place for her in a boarding school in Oklahoma. At age fourteen, speaking no English and knowing no one, Betty Mae started school far from home and family.

For years, she had accompanied her mother, a medicine woman, when she went to deliver babies. Betty Mae was frustrated and sad when the babies died. Surely, she thought, there must be a way to save them. She respected the work of her mother and the medicine men but began to understand their limitations. The burning desire to help influenced her to become the first Seminole to graduate from high school. She then enrolled in nursing school in Oklahoma. Eventually, she headed back to the reservation, establishing a regular circuit among her people. More than once, she was chased by armed medicine men jealously guarding their territory. But in time, as more and more of her patients recovered, her reputation spread, trust grew, and she was often asked to return.

The lovely young woman was pursued by many Seminole men but finally won by Moses Jumper, a World War II hero and alligator wrestler, and they married in 1946. War memories continued to haunt Moses as he fought another lifelong battle, this one with alcohol. When he was unable to wrestle, Betty Mae took his place with the alligators, working for tips to feed her family. The marriage lasted forty-six years, with Betty Mae holding things together, herding cattle, selling crafts, shepherding her two sons and one daughter to church and school, and accepting no excuses from any of them.

When the Seminole tribe received formal recognition in 1957, Betty Mae became the tribe's first vice chairman. In 1967, less than forty years after escaping death at the hands of tribesmen, she ran against three males and won the chairmanship of the tribe. She was the first woman Indian chief in the nation, and she held the position until 1971. When she took office, the tribe's bank balance was about thirty-five dollars; when she left, they had half a million dollars in reserve.

Betty Mae helped found three tribal newspapers, including the respected *Seminole Tribune.* As editor of that paper, she never hesitated to criticize the tribe or the government or lecture young people about drugs or school attendance; in the process, she inspired a legend of her own.

Believing so strongly in education that she pressured not only her own children but any others she thought needed extra encouragement, she gained a reputation as the tribe's unofficial truant officer. She was occasionally seen driving her van through pastures, terrifying cows and truants alike until she nabbed her prey, cleaned them up, and returned them to school.

As Betty Mae was becoming a legend among her own people, she was being recognized by others as well. President Richard Nixon appointed her to a term on the National Indian Opportunity Council. Named among the top fifty Indian women in the United States in 1971, she authored two books and was named "Woman of the Year" by the Jewish Women's Defense League and "Pioneer Woman" by the City of Dania. She was awarded an honorary doctorate of humane letters from Florida State University and was inducted into the Florida Women's Hall of Fame in 1995. The first Lifetime Achievement Award was given to her by the Native American Journalists Association.

Betty Mae was battling her own cancer when she buried her husband of forty-six years, but other awards continue to accumulate.

Florida and the nation owe Great-Uncle Jimmie an award of gratitude for preventing the death of that little girl more than ninety years ago.

1942

Nazis Invade Florida

The bulging Sunday editions of Florida's newspapers welcomed the new tourist season on December 7, 1941, but by late afternoon, the tragedy at Pearl Harbor eclipsed everything already printed. Fear came to the Land of Flowers.

Like the rest of the world, Floridians had been watching storm clouds gather in Europe. After Pearl Harbor, the state speedily transformed itself from tourist mecca to military state. Airfields constructed under the New Deal became military training bases. Flight schools mushroomed in the ideal climate and topography. Hotels, emptied of fearful tourists, overflowed with servicemen and their families. Camp Blanding, south of Jacksonville, expanded to ninety thousand officers and enlistees, becoming the fourth-largest city in Florida. Even relaxed Key West ballooned with personnel needed to manage ship repair and maintenance. Servicemen drilled at Castillo de San Marcos, the stone fort built in 1672 at St. Augustine. Capturing all eyes, the proud women of the recently created Women's Army Corps paraded down the boardwalk in Daytona Beach.

America's entry into the war also cleared the way for German submarines patrolling our eastern seaboard to swiftly switch from observation to an offensive action known as Operation Drumbeat.

On February 19, 1942, the German U-boat ("U" for *Unterseeboot,* "submarine" in German) U-128 torpedoed the US tanker *Pan Massachusetts* off the coast of Cape Canaveral, exploding its one hundred thousand barrels of oil into a flaming colossus, killing twenty of its thirty-eight crew members in front of thousands of terrified civilians onshore. If they had entertained any lingering doubts, Floridians now knew they were at war.

Tankers and freighters carrying munitions and oil up the East Coast joined convoys heading across the North Atlantic, but the US Navy was spread too thin for adequate defense. Deadly attacks continued relentlessly, destroying ships in numbers so shocking that the government hid the truth—two or three ships were being demolished every day.

Observation towers built by the Coast Guard every three miles along the eastern beaches were staffed in shifts by civilians, including Florida author Marjorie Kinnan Rawlings. Subs torpedoed ships day and night in view of horrified civilians, some of whom launched their own small boats in daring rescues of crewmen. Unfortunate beach walkers stumbled on burned corpses washed up on shore while, overhead, women and men in unarmed Civil Air Patrol planes performed dangerous work as spotters.

After Pearl Harbor, under direct orders from Adolf Hitler, an American sabotage program was launched. *Operation Pastorius,* named for the first German immigrant to America, had two goals. The first of these goals was industrial sabotage; metal and power plants and water and railroad facilities in the East were targeted for destruction. The second goal was to incite ill feeling against German Americans, hopefully uniting them in traitorous activity while simultaneously demoralizing Americans.

The first sabotage units dispatched consisted of two groups of four men, all of whom had lived and worked in the United States but had returned to Germany before World War II began. One group of four was assigned to land on Long Island; the other was to go ashore at Ponte Vedra Beach, Florida.

In the Florida group was Edward Kerling, age thirty-three, who had worked in a New York packing plant and as a chauffeur. Harboring an intense dislike for Americans, Kerling became active in the Nazi party when he returned to Germany. Herbert Haupt, age twenty-two, was brought to the United States by his parents when he was five. His father, loyal to the Nazis, influenced Herbert to join the German American Bund, a Nazi organization. Warner Thiel, thirty-five years old, was a toolmaker in Los Angeles, Philadelphia, and Detroit. Herman Newbauer, age thirty-two, a hotel worker in Chicago and Hartford, was sympathetic to the Nazis.

During their two months of training near Berlin, all had learned the fine points of blowing up bridges and everything they needed to know about fuses, detonators, and explosives. American magazines provided a crash course in slang and hit songs. The men received fake IDs and other forged documents at a graduation gala before boarding U-584, heading west across the Atlantic.

Four men landed at the eastern tip of Long Island on June 12, 1942. On June 17, the others rowed ashore at Ponte Vedra Beach, south of Jacksonville, in a rubber inflatable, wearing swimsuits and caps adorned with swastikas, a precaution in case they were captured. (Without military markings, they could be convicted as spies and executed. With military insignias, they could claim to be invaders and demand to be treated as prisoners of war.) Each man wore a money belt holding about seven thousand dollars, and together they pulled along four large waterproof boxes of explosives, detonators, trench shovels, and American suitcases containing American clothing, identification, and a small rubber ball. Landing unnoticed, they buried their boxes in the sand two hundred feet east of Highway AIA, intending to recover them later. They headed north, pretending to be tourists playing ball in the surf and attracting no undue attention. Upon reaching Jacksonville Beach, they donned regular clothes, caught a bus for breakfast in Jacksonville, then split into twosomes and registered at different hotels.

In the morning, Newbauer and Haupt proceeded to Chicago, where they were assisted by Haupt's parents, but they made the mistake of partying with Haupt's old girlfriend and a bartender pal, who promptly turned them in to authorities. They were arrested immediately. Kerling and Thiel traveled to New York City and were nabbed by the Federal Bureau of Investigation (FBI).

The New York group had landed four days before the Florida group, and its leader, Georg Dasch, had within thirty hours exposed the entire operation to the FBI. He tried to buy leniency by claiming sympathy toward America, and he cited circumstances such as pressure from his German mother and coercion from Nazi authorities because of his knowledge about America. Soon, all eight men were in custody.

Handcuffed and in leg irons, Kerling was hauled back to Jacksonville Beach to point out the location of the buried boxes. Not wanting to disrupt the possible landings of other saboteurs, the FBI maintained the strictest secrecy while munitions experts retrieved the explosives from the sand.

A trial was held for all eight men in the Justice Department in Washington, DC, on July 8, 1942. Black curtains covered the windows. The press was excluded. At the end of three weeks, all were pronounced guilty and sentenced to death by electrocution. However, President Roosevelt commuted Dasch's sentence to thirty years at hard labor and another in the New York group, Ernst Burger, to life in prison because of their cooperation. All who aided Haupt in Chicago were arrested, tried, and imprisoned, then deported. Six weeks after landing on American soil, the remaining six saboteurs were electrocuted by the US Army on August 8, 1942, in Washington, DC.

When President Truman approved clemency for Dasch and Burger in 1948, they were deported to Germany. Dasch later published a memoir, *Eight Spies against America,* in which he reiterated his claim of sympathy to America and wrote that the FBI had double-crossed him. His claims were disputed by the FBI, and he was forbidden to return to the United States. He was by then shunned in Germany because he walked free while the others were executed.

The secret was well kept, for it was not until after the war ended that Floridians learned of the nighttime Nazi invasion of 1942.

1951

A Quiet Hero

On Christmas Day in 1951, in the small town of Mims, Florida, at the home of Harry T. and Harriette Moore, the loving couple happily observed their twenty-fifth wedding anniversary. They were joined by Harry's mother, Rosa, and their oldest daughter, Annie Rosalea, also known as Peaches, who was home for the holidays from her teaching job in Ocala. Peaches snuggled on the couch with a book for a while, enjoying the chance to relax. Their younger daughter, Evaline, was expected home from her job in Washington, DC, the next morning.

Harry and the family had celebrated Christmas with his mother, Rosa, at her nearby home. But that afternoon, he still wanted to celebrate his and Harriette's wedding anniversary. Christmas was special, but it was twenty-five years since they married and that was extra special.

At his insistence, Harriette, Rosa, and Peaches all sat down with Harry to enjoy some fruit cake in memory of his and Harriette's wedding. He and his wife joined hands to cut the cake together as he proclaimed his enduring love for her before they all enjoyed their treat. But soon, Harriette, totally exhausted from her very busy day, regretfully excused herself and retired. Peaches, too, was drained, said goodnight, and headed into her bedroom.

Rosa was certainly feeling her age, but she took that time to plead with Harry, as she had so often, to stop the work he was doing with the National Association for the Advancement of Colored People (NAACP). She was terribly afraid that in continuing it, he was seriously endangering his own life. Harry loved his mother, but with all his heart and soul, he was convinced that the work he was doing was for the benefit of their entire race and he could not quit. Finally, at just past ten o'clock, Rosa, tired and sad, said goodnight and slowly made her way to the guest bedroom at the back of the house.

Alone then, Harry turned off all the lights and looked out the window, seeing that a heavy fog had closed in. It had been a good night to stay at home with his family. Quietly, he joined Harriette who was sound asleep in their bed.

It had been five or ten minutes after the foggy nightfall began when two men, who had driven to Mims, turned onto Old Dixie Highway and drove slowly until they reached the deserted driveway they were looking for. They stopped, checking to be sure there were no lights on in the nearby house. When they were satisfied no one was awake in the home, they got out of their car and, using a flashlight, removed a package from the trunk. The shorter man had been there before. He took the package and hurried to the house where he checked the surroundings, then quietly crawled under the house, which was elevated off the ground on cinder blocks. Quickly placing the package on the ground on the specific spot he had decided on, he wriggled back out again and joined his partner. The car with the two men made a speedy getaway.

At 10:20 PM, a monstrous explosion that shook the territory for miles around actually lifted part of the Moores' home off its cinder blocks. The bomb had been placed under the floor directly beneath Harry and Harriette's bed. Amazingly fast, rescuers arrived, dug the couple out of the wreck, and rushed them to the hospital. Harry, critically injured, died on the way. Harriette reached the hospital alive, but in a very serious condition. When sufficiently conscious, she understood that Harry was gone, and though in excruciating pain and with tears flooding her eyes, she prevailed on her daughters to take her to the mortuary. Her own doctor was against it, but the daughters hired an ambulance to take Harriette to see her husband one last time. Somehow, with Rosa's help, they managed it, then insisted on returning her to the hospital. She didn't want to go and tearfully clung to his body. Without Harry, she felt she had no reason to live, but she was unable to hold on and they moved her back to the hospital. She lived for nine more days of anguish and pain before she joined her love.

For seventeen years, Harry T. Moore, who never became really famous, nevertheless had been a hated Black person in Florida. As the coordinator of the NAACP, he traveled alone all over the state in one of three cars, all of which he wore out, investigating lynchings, race crimes against students and teachers in schools, and other covered-up or unsolved crimes.

Also, he was the executive secretary of the Progressive Voters League, and worked tirelessly—he was personally instrumental in registering one hundred thousand Black voters in just six years. When he was at home, he worked hour after hour at his typewriter, writing protests and circulars to send to places where they mattered.

Harry had always been genuinely dedicated to his profession. He was a schoolteacher who, after working for twenty years, was fired for fighting against racial violations long before anyone was aware of how common they were. But that work had taken over Harry's life and he would not, could not stop. "Why would they hate Harry enough to do this?" friends asked when he lost the job. And the answer was almost always one word. "Groveland."

Groveland was a packing house town in southern Lake County, fifty miles from Brevard County where all hell broke loose when, in July 1949, four young Black men were arrested for the rape of a seventeen-year-old White woman. The crime at that time in Florida was ruled to result in the death penalty for the perpetrator. The accused in this case were Walter Irvin, Charles Greenlee, Samuel Shepherd, and Ernest Thomas.

When Harry Moore heard the news, then learned there were no named witnesses, no actual evidence in the case, and that the medical examiner stated he found no actual evidence of a crime, Harry wasted no time getting involved. Also becoming involved was Sherriff Willis McCall, a proud White person, a firm racist and a segregationist, characterizations of him which were well known and never denied by him. A few days after hearing both the facts and rumors of the case, crowds of local residents began roaming the area, bitter and enraged. Hundreds of armed locals were joined by members of the Ku Klux Klan, a heavy influence there. The mob viciously attacked all Black people and destroyed their homes.

Regardless of who related the events of July 16, 1949, basically, the story was that a young married couple, Norma and Willie Padgett, on their way home after a night out, became stuck with car trouble on a deserted country road about fifteen miles north of Groveland, when another car with four young Black men in it stopped, supposedly to help. But the men reportedly knocked Willie out, grabbed Norma, and drove off with her in their car. She later claimed that all four raped her, then drove away, leaving her hiding alone, crying and terrified in the woods until, in the slowly emerging daylight, she was able to see enough to make her way to get help.

Meanwhile, Willie had managed to get his car to a gas station where the worker phoned Lake County Sheriff McCall, who immediately sent two deputies. With Willie's description of the car used by the young Black men, their car was spotted early that morning, parked in front of a nondescript house. The quiet owner of the house told the deputies he had loaned his car to his younger brother and a friend who were there in his home. Called outside, the brother, Shepherd, and his pal, Irwin, were both arrested and amazingly soon, their two friends were both caught, too. Thomas, who was nabbed in the woods 150 miles away after a ten-day hunt, was shot and killed. Sixteen-year-old Greenlee was caught there, too, and arrested when he was found holding a loaded pistol. It was a busy time.

By morning, the front page of every newspaper in Florida carried the story. In no time, a mob of armed White locals roamed the streets of Lake County and were setting fire to

Black-owned homes, setting off alarms and alerting the governor, but getting no responses.

An all-White jury found the three captured men guilty, sentencing Shepherd and Irwin to death and young Greenlee to life in prison. The sentences were ironic in that the medical examiner had concluded that Norma Padgett had not been raped. Harry Moore wasted no time inciting a campaign that the convictions were improper and incorrect.

In the meantime, Sherriff McCall had been driving the handcuffed Shepherd and Irwin to the Lake County jail, and later claimed that when he had to stop the car to check an apparent problem with his tires, they tried to attack him. He shot them both, killing Shepherd instantly. Irwin survived, but when Harry Moore called on authorities for McCall to be investigated for shooting Shepherd, Harry was ignored and McCall was never accused. Of course, there had been no witnesses.

Still, Harry continued working hard for the NAACP, but with their dues having doubled, the group was losing members at a fast rate. Harry constantly drove around the state trying to stop the loss and increase the number of members. He worked hour after hour teaching Black Floridians how important their vote was and how it was necessary to follow the strict rules to ensure their vote was counted.

He also started to carry a pistol, both because of the increasing number of threats he was receiving mostly by mail, but also because their house was once broken into when he and Harriette had been away. Closets and drawers were left messy, and Harry's shotgun was gone, the one that he used for killing snakes and other such intruders.

Sadly, when the annual national meeting of the Florida State Conference of the NAACP was held in November, despite Harry's heartfelt plea, it was decided that they could no longer afford to pay his salary, and his position was abolished. He was named to be the "state coordinator," unpaid except for actual expenses of the position.

Downcast but determined, and despite the concerns of his family and friends for him, Harry went on. "I'm going to keep doing it, even if it costs me my life," he said. And it did.

On Christmas night in 1951, it cost him his life.

1956

A Small Patch of Cuba

Regardless of whether we ought to be there, the US Naval Base at Guantanamo is to most Americans a small piece of the United States on Cuban soil. Lesser known is the fact that a patch of the Communist nation exists in one of Florida's great cities.

From the time the mortally wounded Juan Ponce de León departed Florida for Cuba, no other state in the union has been so affected by the island country ninety miles from US shores as has Florida. Reverberations from Cuba's struggle for independence from Spain in the 1800s extended great distances, especially to the cigar-making enclaves of Key West and Tampa, both flourishing Latin communities. Many Floridians thought of Cuba as an outpost of Florida; some Cubans considered Florida an outpost of Cuba.

When Vincente Martinez Ybor moved his cigar factory from Key West to Tampa in the mid-1880s, it was the beginning of a population explosion and of what would become the "Cigar Capital of the World," the unique Ybor City. There, Cuban exiles created vibrant nationalist societies working passionately for the liberation of Cuba: *Cuba Libre!* While the men headed political and propaganda organizations, women organized fund-raising events—fiestas, parades, picnics—and collected contributions door-to-door. Women donated everything from silver tea sets to homemade crafts; they sold or raffled the items and gave the proceeds to the cause. Women and men who held jobs donated one day's pay.

Four years after Ybor City was incorporated into the municipality of Tampa, José Martí, the "Apostle of Cuban Liberty," arrived at midnight in the driving rain at the Ybor City railroad station, eager to connect with and thank his loyal followers. Martí, a small, sad-eyed man with a gift for spellbinding oratory, was also a writer, teacher, and propagandist who worked not only for political independence from Spain but also for social justice and the end of racism and all forms of oppression in Cuba. As early as 1892, he wrote unusual sentiments for the times: "that the campaigns of a people are only weak, when they do not recruit the heart of a woman; but when the woman rallies and helps . . . the project is invincible." Martí returned again and again to Ybor City, strengthened by the outpouring of support he received there.

One of the outstanding Ybor City women who championed Martí and Cuban independence was Paulina Pedrosa, an Afro-Cuban émigré. She managed a boardinghouse at 8th Avenue and 12th Street to accommodate the many unmarried men who worked in the cigar factories with her husband,

Ruperto. Relatives living nearby joined with the Pedrosas and like-minded friends, responding to Martí's eloquence with organized activities in support of a free Cuba.

Paulina was tireless in her enthusiasm for the cause, and Martí regarded her as a special friend, walking arm-in-arm with her about the neighborhood. However, as time went on, it became more difficult for Martí to raise money in the United States. Spain sent spies to Ybor City to undermine his efforts, some working in the cigar factories, planting seeds of doubt as to his honesty among the citizenry. Workers began to distrust him. At one appearance, when his entry was greeted with little enthusiasm, a voice in the crowd called him a bandit, and, for a moment, no one came to his defense. Among the mostly male audience was the redoubtable Paulina Pedrosa, who strode to the front of the room, angrily shouting, "If any of you is afraid to give his money ... let him give me his pants and I'll give him my petticoat!" The men laughed sheepishly, then applauded as the grateful Martí hugged his friend.

From the time of his first visit to Ybor City, a room had always been reserved for Martí at Rubiera Hotel, but as his fame spread, it became more and more difficult for the frail Martí to rest and escape the constant, though well-intentioned, interruptions. On one particular day, following his afternoon appearance at the cigar factory, he accepted the invitation of two admiring Cubans to stay with them at their house in order to avoid the crowds. The arrangement proved satisfactory until his hosts went out one afternoon and he sampled the wine they left for him. He thought it smelled peculiar when he touched it to his lips. He spat it out, but when his doctor came by on a routine visit a little later, he found his famous patient feeling weak and faint. The doctor promptly instituted treatment, strongly suspecting that the homeowners were Spanish agents who had poisoned the wine. Martí recovered, but the doctor's suspicions seemed to be confirmed when the two Cuban men disappeared.

Word traveled like a flash through the community. Just as speedily, Paulina Pedrosa arrived, swept into Rubiera Hotel, gathered up Martí and his things, and moved them all to the house she shared with Ruperto. From that time on, there was no discussion; it was understood that Martí stayed with them, and the Pedrosas flew the Cuban flag from the gable of their house when he was in town. Émigrés kept a vigil outside in the street, hoping for a glimpse of the revered "El Maestro," watching the candle glow in his window where he worked at his desk. The Pedrosas took personal responsibility for his security during his stays, with Ruperto sleeping on the floor in front of Martí's door to ensure his safety at night. Paulina nursed Martí back to health when he fell ill from exhaustion. After they had already donated almost all their worldly goods to the cause of *Cuba Libre!*, they sold their small house, which they had acquired at great sacrifice, and gave the proceeds to the cause.

Before independence from Spain could be secured, Martí was assassinated by Spanish soldiers in Cuba, plunging Ybor City into mourning.

Paulina and Ruperto returned to a free Cuba in 1910, having struggled financially in the aftermath of a bitter strike in the Ybor City cigar factories. In honor of their service to the cause, the Cuban government provided them with a rent-free house. Ruperto was given a doorman's job, and Paulina, who was going blind, received a small pension.

Today in the heart of Ybor City is a small piece of land that belongs to the government of Cuba. At 8th Avenue and

13th Street, near where the little Pedrosa house once stood, the Park of the Friends of José Martí was created in his memory in 1956. When it was being built by the Ybor City Rotary Club, the club had difficulty raising the last twenty-five thousand dollars. A delegation traveled to Cuba, and during a meeting with then Cuban President Fulgencio Batista, they explained their predicament. "It is an honor to contribute to the memory of the Apostle of Liberty," Batista said. "The twenty-five thousand dollars is yours."

And so, the site was deeded to the government of Cuba and still technically belongs to that country. Although her home burned down, a nearby plaque honors Paulina Pedrosa as "one of the great women patriots of Cuba."

1962

Cuban Missile Crisis

Twenty-five Naval Air Station trucks lumbered through downtown Jacksonville, delivering supplies to buildings clearly marked "Nuclear Fallout Shelters." Scuttlebutt had Jacksonville at the top of the Soviets' list of targets. Children all over the state practiced what to do if the missiles came. They watched their dads build bomb shelters in the backyard, knowing that if the bad guys had their way, Florida would be wiped off the map.

In 1962, the Cold War, which had been heating up, reached a frightening level. On October 14, two US Air Force high-flying U-2 reconnaissance aircraft, at times flying at treetop height, took photos in Cuba that confirmed that bases for intermediate missiles were being constructed at breakneck speed. Rumors had long circulated within Cuba about a possible US invasion or assassination of Cuban Communist leader Fidel Castro. However, in the minds of President John F. Kennedy and his advisers, Soviet Premier Nikita Khrushchev was attempting to alter the balance of power in the Cold War by building bases in Cuba and by arming Cubans—ultimately moving weapons closer to the United States.

Clearly, forty missiles were already in place, aimed at the United States, able to reach as far as Washington, DC. Under construction were bases for missiles able to destroy US cities from coast to coast. Additional film showed twenty-five bombers capable of carrying nuclear bombs. Twenty-five ships sped through the Atlantic toward Cuba, loaded with more missiles and bombers.

Military experts estimated that within minutes of the firing of Cuban missiles, eighty million Americans would be dead. Quality of life for survivors was not openly discussed.

Decisions engendering possibly the most catastrophic consequences in the history of the world needed to be made by a handful of people with utmost secrecy and speed. Some experts favored immediate air and ground strikes. Some opted for political action accompanied by diplomacy. Others believed that open surveillance and a blockade of offensive weapons entering Cuba was preferable. The last option was chosen by the commander in chief, President Kennedy, and announced at six o'clock on the evening of October 22 on national television to a solemn nation. "Should these offensive military preparations continue," he said, "I have directed the armed forces to prepare for any eventuality."

The country overwhelmingly backed their young president, as did US allies in the North Atlantic Treaty Organization (NATO) and the Organization of American States (OAS).

The world held its breath, but nowhere was the crisis felt more acutely than in Florida. The state was a twenty-minute flight from Cuban shores and was expected to be either the staging area for a Cuban invasion or first to be hit by Soviet missiles.

The Florida National Guard was put on twenty-four-hour alert. Nervous citizens heard Florida described as the Achilles' heel of American air defenses. Every submarine at Boca Chica base in Key West was sent to sea as the normally laid-back town converted to an armed camp. Marines with guns mingled with beachgoers on the sand as antiaircraft missiles were sped to Boca Chica and into the Everglades. Men chosen to establish these new missile sites were rushed in without much equipment and forced to live in tents, bathe in canals, and do battle with mosquitoes.

Meanwhile, amid fear and confusion, Florida families stocked up on bottled water and canned goods, seriously considering the frenzied pitch of door-to-door salesmen selling bomb shelters. No one was sure exactly what was happening, but Orlando City Hall stocked emergency provisions, the same as they did for Hurricane Donna. Secrecy was so strict that one Orlando reporter was arrested for trying to uncover facts at McCoy Air Force Base. Tampa sporting goods stores had a run on shotguns and rifles. Only in Miami, where the train yards were filled with military equipment, was there any joy. It seemed that along Calle Ocho some Cubans believed they would be home in two days. It would be the end of Fidel, they confidently predicted.

Especially for children, it was a scary time to live in Florida. Squadrons of supersonic F-100s and F-06s tore out of Patrick and MacDill Air Force Bases at all hours. While U-2s flew from McCoy in Orlando, air force bases in Tampa,

Orlando, and Satellite Beach were on high alert, and low-level reconnaissance planes zoomed out of MacDill in Tampa. Kids could hardly look up without seeing military aircraft.

Frightened parents tearfully whispered among themselves about how far children would get if they ran home from school, and men worried that they wouldn't make it from work to their families "in time." Debates raged about bomb shelters and the ethics of refusing entry to neighbors in order to sustain family members for a longer time. One man taught his children a gruesome lesson in how to use the body bags he stocked and how to dispose of bodies in case the children outlasted their parents. Families invented secret knocks to enter, keeping strangers out of their shelters. Some shelters were elaborate, with heavy, steel doors, bulletproof glass, and secret escape hatches.

Duval County children were issued dog tags, marked "P" for Protestant, "J" for Jewish, or "C" for Catholic, just in case. Most Florida elementary schools had student survival packs in citrus bags hung on designated hooks. Each pack contained canned food, bandages, and a bottle of bleach to purify drinking water after the missiles fell.

Throughout the rest of the country, people watched and prayed. Churches remained open all night, where citizens prayed for peace and for civilization not to end. The few attempts at gallows humor—"See you tomorrow, if there is a tomorrow"—fell flat. Most people were glued to their televisions, reassured by Walter Cronkite's calm presence.

A day and a half after President Kennedy ordered the blockade, the first Soviet ship was intercepted, inspected, and allowed to proceed. Sixteen hours later, a freighter was permitted to go on, but more important, in another part of the Atlantic, Soviet ships bound for Cuba stopped, turned, and headed home. The blockade was successful, but the missiles were still in Cuba.

While continuing the military buildup, the United States pressed Khrushchev through the United Nations. There, in probably his finest hour, US Ambassador Adlai Stevenson demanded that the Soviet ambassador admit before the world the placing of offensive weapons in Cuba. Prepared to wait for an answer "until hell freezes over," Stevenson displayed undisputable evidence with photos taken by the Light Photographic Squadron 62 out of Cecil Field near Jacksonville. Those pilots would each receive the Distinguished Flying Cross for skimming over the ocean to Cuba in single-pilot, unarmed Crusader aircraft, maintaining radio silence as they searched out their reconnaissance targets, took photos, and then tore out into international waters where they were met by armed escorts, hopefully before being met by Soviet planes.

Although Khrushchev had ordered that no US surveillance planes were to be shot down, a Soviet commander, in violation of that order, shot down a US Air Force plane on October 27. This action provided the Soviet premier with irrefutable evidence that the crisis was spinning out of control. The game of chicken could obviously lead to the destruction of all humankind.

When Khrushchev received Kennedy's letter insisting that no settlement could be reached until all missiles were removed from Cuba, he responded one day later with a mild reply, expressing "satisfaction and gratitude for the sense of proportion and understanding of the responsibility borne by you for the preservation of peace throughout the world, which you have shown."

Kennedy answered within hours, welcoming Khrushchev's "statesmanlike decision." The world breathed again. Floridians believed they had a clearer realization than the rest of the country of how terrifyingly close the world came to annihilation.

1967

Dr. Cade Wins the Orange Bowl

In the early 1960s, over a cup of coffee with a football coach, Dr. Robert Cade first considered the implications of the enormous amounts of perspiration lost by football players during a game. The professor of physiology at the University of Florida in Gainesville learned that, whether playing up north in the snow or at home under the blazing Florida sun, a player could lose as much as eighteen pounds of body weight in one game early in the season. He knew that no more than a half pound of fat could be burned by that amount of exercise, and with no bathroom breaks (none were ever needed) the extraordinary weight loss had to be due to perspiration.

But what other vital elements were being lost along with the perspiration? A check of existing records revealed no information on the subject, and the doctor was intrigued.

With permission from Head Coach Ray Graves to run tests on the freshman team, Dr. Cade launched his study. (The Gators varsity was not to be experimented on, the two men agreed.)

The players' sweat was measured for volume and concentrations of sodium, potassium, protein, glucose, and other elements, plus changes in volumes before, during, and after games. Among other things, Dr. Cade and his assistants learned that as the players' blood volume falls early on, no blood is pumped to the skin for cooling. Sweat drips off, lowering blood volume even more. As the cycle progresses, blood flow to the skin becomes almost nil. The same condition continues on to the muscles, then to the brain.

With loss of perspiration, sodium in the blood goes up. Normal serum sodium is 140, and if it rises to just 150, many people become confused. At 155, almost everyone is confused, responding with difficulty to external stimuli, such as a cranky 265-pound linebacker wearing the wrong-colored jersey, looming ahead.

Tests showed players were also burning sugar, sometimes lowering their blood sugar to as low as the forties. Normal blood sugar is 80 to 120, and as any diabetic can testify, a blood sugar level in the forties would make one shaky, weak, clammy, and, again, mentally slower and confused, a benefit to opposing football goliaths.

Dr. Cade had found three enormously important factors, each of which could have devastating effects on the abilities of a football player. For the brilliant physiology professor, the solution was self-evident—a mixture containing needed amounts of sugar and salt ingested in time to prevent the undesirable effects of heavy perspiring, but in amounts that would not affect functioning of the gastrointestinal tract.

Coach Graves gave his go-ahead to try the solution on the freshmen during a Friday afternoon scrimmage with a B team the day before a varsity game with Louisiana State University.

After an unremarkable first half ended with the B team ahead 13–0, the mystery-fueled freshmen so dominated the second half that one University of Florida player begged the opposing team to play another quarter, it was so much fun.

The impressed coach approved supplying the magic beverage to the varsity team.

That evening, Dr. Cade and his aides raided every physiology lab at the university to find enough glucose to cook up their precious recipe. They refrigerated the solution overnight, carted it onto the field in a wagon on Saturday afternoon, and passed it out to the players along the sidelines. Without going into the exact wording, suffice it to say that the liquid elicited somewhat rude descriptions as to its taste.

Although the Gators won by only a single point, they had been down 13–0 at the end of the first half and had come back to outplay Louisiana State University in the second half, allowing just one first down and no more points. From that time on, Coach Graves reversed the popular policy of the day that prohibited drinks on the field. Dr. Cade's magic potion would thereafter be a permanent fixture at all Gator games.

Attempts to improve the foul taste of the concoction with lemon-lime flavoring didn't work well, the result tasting too much like turpentine. To correct that problem, Dr. Cade sent all the way to Bologna, Italy, for a special extract he heard about that sold for eighteen dollars a gallon. When it was delivered, the doctor learned it had been made in the town of Frostproof, Florida, and was available in the United States for one dollar a gallon.

Meanwhile, word about the exceptional results from the use of the drink, officially called Gatorade, was spreading. Gatorade was being packaged in milk cartons at the university's dairy science lab. At the last game of that season, played in Miami, a newspaper reporter noticed empty milk cartons lying on the ground and started asking questions. No, the players weren't drinking milk, he was told. It was Gatorade. The first story on the miracle drink appeared in the *Miami Herald* and from there its fame mushroomed.

Successes were repeated over and over, proving it was not a fluke. In the 1967 Orange Bowl, when the Gators outplayed Georgia Tech with flashy moves by Heisman trophy winner Steve Spurrier and a ninety-four-yard run by Larry Smith, the reputation of Dr. Cade's invention was sealed. Georgia Tech's coach, Bobby Dodds, commented after the game, "We didn't have Gatorade—that made the difference." Dr. Cade became known as the only physiology professor ever credited with winning the Orange Bowl.

In addition, Gatorade became the top moneymaker among the patented products developed by University of Florida research, providing millions of dollars to support other research and endowments.

Gatorade was far from the only thing on Dr. Robert Cade's scientific mind. A supporter of education at all levels, he found time to substitute teach at an elementary school during a teachers' strike. He enjoyed working closely with medical students as he focused on kidney and liver disease, rheumatoid arthritis, lupus, hypertension, and diabetes. He took pleasure in his good doctor-patient relationships and often worked in his lab to search for solutions to other medical problems.

In 1997, Dr. Cade and his wife, Mary, sponsored building some badly needed cabins and funding several scholarships at the Florida Camp for Children and Youth with Diabetes. In 1999, they endowed a professorship of physiology at the University of Florida College of Medicine, a payback, Dr. Cade said, for his first job.

The indefatigable doctor, who played violin and viola, was long involved in music in his community and supported the University of Florida Orchestra and the Gainesville Symphony Orchestra, funding thirty scholarships for music students.

In addition to teaching and conducting research at the University of Florida, he enjoyed tending his hybrid rose garden and his collection of Studebakers. Among Dr. Cade's awards and honors are the Florida Governor's Leadership Award, a Worldwide Recognition Development honor, and a Distinguished Service Award from the University of Florida. He was named Outstanding Clinical Professor five times at the University of Florida.

But by far, Dr. Cade's best-known claim to fame is Gatorade, now a staple at sporting events worldwide.

He retired from the university in 2004 and died in 2007.

1971

Tired Housewife from Micanopy

Spanish explorers had barely landed when the idea surfaced to slice Florida in half by constructing a canal to provide ships with a shortcut to the West Coast. This would allow sailors who feared the strange and terrifying southern tip of the Florida peninsula to bypass its treacherous coral reefs and fierce storms at sea and its hostile Indians and alligators on land. Over the years, the idea was studied exhaustively, inspiring one US congressman in the 1820s to claim he would "not think it much of a loss to the United States were the whole Peninsula of Florida sunk into the Gulf of Mexico." During the Great Depression, the project was resurrected by President Franklin Roosevelt to create badly needed jobs. It was halted once more when hydrologists doubted the canal could be constructed without damaging the Florida aquifer and causing contamination of drinking water for central and north Florida. The project ended after ten months with just 3 percent of the canal finished and at a cost of $5.5 million.

The proposed canal, which always failed to meet a projected cost-benefit ratio, was revived again during World War II as a shallower barge canal. However, building materials were needed for the war and unavailable for civilian use, so the idea was once again scrapped.

After the war, Florida development exploded, with new residents arriving in droves. Soon it was hard to find any part of Florida unchanged from what had attracted everyone in the first place. The spring-fed Ocklawaha River, meandering through 110 miles of moss-draped, semitropical forests, with canopies of cypress and sabal palms, was one place that had escaped the developers' hands. No neon signs, no waterfront condos, not a gas pump in sight.

But in 1962, pushed by Jacksonville business interests, Congress appropriated funds and, like the phoenix rising from the ashes, the barge canal idea once more sprang to life. A sixteen-mile section of the Ocklawaha River, pronounced the "sweetest water lane in the world" by one poet, was dammed, summarily destroying nine thousand acres of its floodplain hardwood forest. A huge crawler-crusher smashed hundreds of thousands of trees, turning one of Florida's most beautiful, rich ecosystems into shallow, weed-filled Rodman Pool, whose warm, still waters quickly filled with invasive water lettuce, hyacinths, and algae. The same monstrous contraption that felled the hardwood forest also chipped into the limestone, threatening the upper aquifer and laying waste to species of plants on the endangered list while gutting the habitat of untold animals, birds, and fish.

Rodman Pool, renamed Lake Ocklawaha by the Army Corps of Engineers, was first touted as a fisherman's paradise. It was naturally well stocked by bass from the Ocklawaha River, but as it turned into a rancid marsh, fishing slacked off, requiring the Corps to spend substantial funds on research, poisons, and mechanical removal of the invasive plants. Species of fish slowly died off, but there were also several major fish kills resulting from low oxygen levels. Manatees were killed in the lock and adjoining structures. The dam project was a disaster by almost any criterion. Still, it was resolutely defended in the legislature by some sportfishermen and tournament organizers, as well as a few duck hunters and their supporters.

Margaret Mead famously said, "Never doubt that a small group of thoughtful, committed citizens can change the world. Indeed, it is the only thing that ever has." The words seem tailored to a group led by Marjorie Harris Carr, a self-described "tired old housewife from Micanopy," who was president of the Alachua County Audubon Society, wife of naturalist Archie Carr, and mother of five. An ecologist in her own right, Marjorie loathed controversy but realized something had to be done. She spearheaded "a small group of thoughtful, committed citizens" in a decades-long, determined lobbying and educational effort to save the Ocklawaha River.

In 1969, the Alachua County Audubon Society joined others—hydrologists, economists, lawyers, zoologists, geologists, and other scientists—to form the Florida Defenders of the Environment (FDE) to cooperate with the Environmental Defense Fund (the reversed initials were deliberately chosen) in stopping construction of the Cross Florida Barge Canal and restoring the Ocklawaha River. The alliance of scientific specialists, intent on getting the facts, effectively educated the public, press, and government. Publication by the FDE of a 117-page, carefully researched environmental impact report was a motivating force behind the formation of the National Environmental Policy Act.

The report was also instrumental in President Richard Nixon's 1971 decision to order a halt to canal construction, citing potential environmental damage. But despite support from five presidents, most of Florida's US representatives, its US senators, and a majority of the Florida legislature, a few northern Florida congressmen (one of whom was on the Appropriations Committee) managed to stop de-authorization of the canal—with an estimated cost of over twenty million dollars of taxpayers' money.

Marjorie Carr and the FDE were encouraged by the cessation of work but would not rest until the Rodman Dam was removed and the river restored. They stressed that such removal would eliminate the enormous costs of managing the new Rodman "ecosystem" and that the free-flowing Ocklawaha would never require maintenance, a projected savings of twenty million dollars over twenty years.

Through the years, Marjorie clung to the principle of arriving at environmental rules based on accepted scientific principles, sticking to facts without resorting to emotional assaults. A refined, articulate speaker, Marjorie could fill a room with her laugh, then demolish the opposition with her knowledge of the issues.

"I am an optimist," she said. "I also believe that Floridians care about their environment. If they are educated about its perils, if they are never lied to, they will become stewards of the wild places that are left."

In 1990, the federal canal project was de-authorized by the US Congress, the land reverted to Florida, and efforts to restore the river moved into high gear. But again and again and yet again, efforts were blocked by a few northern Florida legislators. To "honor" one state senator who was tireless in defense of the boondoggle, the dam's name was changed from Rodman to Kirkpatrick Dam.

Finally, in July 2000, conservationists had something to cheer. Governor Jeb Bush announced his support for restoration of the Ocklawaha River by breaching the Kirkpatrick Dam.

The land purchased for the canal was converted to the Marjorie Harris Carr Cross Florida Greenway, an almost continuous span of breathtaking wilderness that stretches from the Atlantic to the Gulf, preserved in perpetuity for nature lovers.

Marjorie, Florida's First Lady of Rivers, passed away on October 10, 1997. Many fondly remember her pacing as she spoke, almost unable to contain her passion as she described the human need for such places as the wild Ockalawaha River. She once said:

> I believe that our difficulty in stating our needs succinctly and persuasively can be attributed to the curious way in which we use our natural environment. For those who go hunting, fishing, boating, or camping, the task of describing what they want from wilderness is easier. These people actively do something to, or in, a natural area. For the people I represent it is enough just to be in wild places. Indeed, some advocates of more tangible activities have accused us of not using wilderness at all. Millions and millions of us do. The original landscapes of America bring us great delight, and we will defend our attitude with increasing vigor.

1971

How the Mouse Got His Kingdom

At a glittering dinner party in St. Louis, local movers and shakers giddily awaited an announcement from Walt Disney himself that the magic of Disney would be coming to their city along with a much-needed bump to its economy.

Amid the evening's gaiety, one intemperate remark from the city's leading business tycoon silenced the congenial chattering. Augustus Busch, scion of the Busch beer family, audibly questioned the sanity of anyone who thought he could build a successful attraction in St. Louis without serving beer or liquor. Challenging the business judgment of one of the world's greatest showmen was not wise. Walt Disney, convinced that beer and theme parks shouldn't be mixed, also believed he knew more about running theme parks than someone who had inherited a beer business. The deal was dead. The quest for a perfect setting for the proposed Magic Kingdom continued.

Walt Disney was searching for a setting that would surpass the site he had selected for Disneyland. Shortly after opening Disneyland in California in 1955, Walt knew he'd made a big mistake. Immediately, others had snatched up surrounding real estate, cramming it with fast-food vendors, cheap souvenir stands, and seedy motels. Right then, Walt decided that any future attractions would include enough surrounding land to provide an insulating greenway, allowing guests to totally escape the real world.

The search proceeded, secret except to Walt, his brother, Roy, and a few trusted associates. If word leaked, available land prices would skyrocket.

Back in California, Walt resumed sketching park plans in a windowless room adjoining his office, a room that had only one key—his.

As reports concerning other possible building sites came back from his team, Florida looked better and better. The climate was nearly perfect, enormous sections of land in the center of the state were used for nothing but cattle grazing, and the state's easy accessibility to the eastern half of the United States was a plus. Walt decided to see it for himself.

He and his group traveled under assumed names, and the easily recognized Walt never left the plane at refueling stops. Flying over Orlando, he made out east-west Interstate 4, under construction where it would intersect with the north-south Florida Turnpike. To the east was McCoy Air Force Base, where civilian flights had started three years earlier. Consequently, the area had excellent accessibility.

"That's it," Walt decided, kicking off an operation so secret it rivaled a Le Carré spy novel.

In carrying out "Project X," as they called it, more than fifty individual land transactions were made through dummy companies, some of them named Retlaw (Walter spelled backwards) Enterprises, Tomahawk Properties, and Latin American Development Company. New York counsel "Wild Bill" Donovan, a former chief in the Office of Strategic Services (forerunner of the Central Intelligence Agency during World War II), provided advice and pulled strings. As land parcels sold, locals buzzed with rumors about who was buying up twenty-four thousand acres at $180 per acre. Guesses included the Ford Motor Company and Howard Hughes, but the purchaser remained a mystery. The final price was a bit over five million dollars for forty-three square miles, an area about twice the size of Manhattan island. Then the story was released.

Orlando Sentinel headlines screamed, "Disney is here!"

Secrecy paid off. After the announcement, the price for an acre of land bounced to eighty thousand dollars, eventually reaching three hundred thousand dollars when the Magic Kingdom opened in 1971.

If acquiring land for a fair price was a coup, Disney officials' next move was a triumph. The Florida governor and legislature acquiesced to Disney demands for creation of a special jurisdiction, the Reedy Creek Improvement District, named for the creek that runs through the area. This gave the corporation the power of an independent municipality—an unprecedented measure affording Disney control over taxation, security and fire departments, public utilities, and building and zoning codes. Rollins College professor Richard Foglesong described the jurisdiction as "the Vatican with mouse ears." The few murmured objections to zoning control and building codes were dismissed by Disney spokesmen who declared such controls necessary since they were proposing an enormous project using cutting-edge construction methods and state-of-the-art technology. One commented, "How else could you build Cinderella's Castle?" With resistance at a minimum, the measure passed and work began in 1969.

Walt, who strongly believed in environmental preservation, committed to setting aside at least seventy-five hundred acres to be kept in their natural state and to draining swampy areas without damaging delicate ecology.

Bay Lake was drained of its unattractive brownish water, the muck that lined its bottom scooped up and combined with the seven million cubic yards of dirt dug up to enlarge the lake. Muck and dirt were used to elevate the theme park twelve feet higher than its surroundings. Bay Lake was relined, refilled with attractive bluish water, and stocked with fish.

Refusing to dig forty miles of canals in customary straight lines, Walt ordered them curved like natural rivers. Hundreds of huge trees were moved rather than cut down, and a tree farm for the cultivation of thousands of trees and other plants and flowers was established.

Experts created an innovative telephone system, using underground cables and the first commercial fiber optic network. The most advanced electric, sewage, and water systems were installed, all controlled by a leading-edge computer system.

Future guests would not realize they were strolling on top of a bustling center of activity. Before starting construction of the Magic Kingdom, a nine-acre world of rooms, halls, and offices was fashioned into what became an underground support system for utilities, storage, dressing rooms, rest areas for employees, shops for maintenance services, electrical and plumbing centers, design and recording facilities, and an employee cafeteria.

The world's largest working wardrobe was crafted to supply costumes for living and animated figures. The world's largest laundry facility was built to wash every costume daily, along with napkins and other linens.

Another first was the installation of automated vacuum assisted collection, a waste system in which trash is collected and whisked away at sixty miles per hour every fifteen minutes through pneumatic tubes to a central compactor. Similarly, a monorail system was built to whisk guests around the park.

Construction aboveground started in 1970 with Main Street, U.S.A., Adventureland, Frontierland, Liberty Square, Fantasyland, and Tomorrowland laid out in spokelike fashion. Builders paid painstaking attention to detail, beginning first with sketches followed by scale models in order to consider appearance from every angle. Workers procured props by the thousands, added rides, and installed audio and special effects, all programmed by computers. Since castle builders are scarce in the United States, constructing Cinderella's Castle was an interesting, 189-foot-high challenge. Additionally, Disney workers built Florida's tallest "mountain"—the 197-foot Big Thunder Mountain—using 650 tons of steel, 4,675 tons of "mud," and 9,000 gallons of paint.

Non-Disney estimates predicted a crowd of one hundred thousand for opening day, October 1, 1971, and extra troopers reported for duty. When just ten thousand guests arrived at the park that day, Disney executives professed to be delighted. With no major problems, minor ones were addressed quickly. Attendance gradually increased, and by

Thanksgiving of that year, parking lots filled early and had to be closed.

Within a few years, Walt Disney World became the nation's leading tourist destination and, shortly thereafter, the world's. One survey showed that 70 percent of all Americans had visited the park, while 60 percent had been to Washington, DC.

1974

The Last Straw

Roxcy Bolton was used to controversy, accustomed to being belittled, humiliated, called names. *Scrappy, hero, stateswoman*—she liked those titles. But *crank, aging dragon, darned fool,* and other even-less-complimentary labels were also hurled her way. It wasn't always easy, but if the names bothered her, she seldom let it show as she went about the noisy business of pioneering for women's rights in southern Florida.

Born a genteel Southern woman, Roxcy learned early on that gentility and white gloves had to be set aside when doors needed to be kicked in. It was 1956 when she first heard Eleanor Roosevelt speak and saw what a determined woman could accomplish. So began a lifetime of activism in which no cause was too small, no person too insignificant, to merit Roxcy's attention.

As a resident of Coral Gables, Roxcy regularly attended city commission meetings, buttonholing public officials, speaking up with passion and humor. When the mayor once threatened to have her arrested and removed from the meeting, she responded, "Go for it," calmly continuing with what she had to say. Her wisecracks and fiery comments made some people snicker before Roxcy's stern look brought the room to silence. "I hope you're laughing with me," she'd say.

When Roxcy began her career as an activist, she helped destitute mothers get child support, assisted a bag lady who slept and finally died on the steps of a Miami church, and went to bat for a woman whose job was threatened by a younger worker with better connections. When she learned of the inhumane conditions Haitian women endured at the Krome Detention Center, she publicly threatened to take the issue to the United Nations, resulting in improvements within twenty-four hours.

In 1966, Roxcy joined with twelve other women to launch the Dade County chapter of the National Organization for Women, supporting candidates favorable to women's issues such as child care for the poor, equal pay, elimination of sex-segregated classified ads in newspapers, and maternity leave for pregnant airline stewardesses rather than the standard pink slips.

In 1969, Roxcy took on some of Miami's major department stores. Male customers in the "men only" sections of their restaurants received fast service, allowing them to return quickly to their important jobs. Women, including businesswomen also in need of fast service, stood in long lines while they looked longingly at empty seats in the men's section. It was the ultimate insult to the bulk of department store customers who were, of course, women. When polite letters of complaint failed to produce changes, the women, referred to as "Roxcy and her dolls" by one male columnist, removed their gloves. They threatened to picket, planning to supply tuna sandwiches to would-be diners standing in lines. Roxcy sealed the argument. "But men and women sleep together," she said. "Why can't they eat together?" The department stores caved in.

It was a triumph. But women won what would be an even more significant victory in 1972 when President Richard Nixon, at Roxcy's relentless prodding, proclaimed August 26 as Women's Equality Day in commemoration of women gaining the right to vote. In a note written to her, Florida's Senator Edward Gurney said that without Roxcy there would be no Women's Equality Day. Of course, success was sweet, but the work went on.

Even in the 1970s, "polite" society did not openly discuss many of the issues of the day affecting women, including domestic violence. Roxcy was instrumental in founding Women in Distress, Florida's first shelter for abused women. Another thing not openly discussed and not supposed to happen to "nice" women was the crime of rape. Roxcy got people to talk about it. To bring it into public consciousness, she helped organize Dade's first Rape Task Force to participate in a march down Flagler Street in 1971. Hoping for fifty marchers, she was pleased when one hundred women showed up.

In a letter to the Miami sheriff and director of public safety, she demanded that police reevaluate their attitude regarding rape, saying there was only one issue of importance: "the woman's body was invaded!" If a woman got off work late at night, had to ride the bus home, and was raped, people would say, "Why was she there at 11:30 at night?"

"A man robbed and beaten in downtown Miami at 11:00 PM does not have to explain why he was there," Roxcy said. "A woman must always explain and prove her innocence when raped. Why? Because the prevailing male attitude is rather cavalier toward rape."

Until Roxcy intervened, victims were quizzed for hours at the scene or at the police station by mostly male officers before receiving medical attention. "Police officers can no longer say they know best how to deal with rape," Roxcy informed the sheriff. "We intend to say how it is best for you to deal with this crime." What Roxcy and the task force wanted was a rape treatment center located at a downtown hospital where victims would be taken immediately and treated by a sensitive, knowledgeable staff. But officials took no action toward this goal.

The last straw came in 1974. The frantic mother of a seventeen-year-old rape victim telephoned Roxcy from the hospital where the girl had been refused admittance. The victim had been referred instead to the Dade County medical examiner's office, the office in charge of autopsies. The underage, traumatized young victim of a heinous crime was examined by a physician trained in handling dead bodies.

Like marines hitting the beach, the outraged Roxcy rallied her task force, badgering every public official at every opportunity, pleading and demanding a hospital-based treatment center. The support of County Manager Ray Goode and Dade County State Attorney Dick Gerstein led to the Dade County Commission unanimously passing legislation to establish a rape treatment center at Jackson Memorial Hospital. It was the first such center in the nation.

The Rape Treatment Center, which opened in January 1974, received a letter of thanks from Roxcy, who said, "A

Rape Center at the County's hospital can best be classified as a part of the Marshall Plan for WOMANKIND—It's overdue!!" She continued, "The ravages woman's body and mind has suffered in this country is indeed equal to suffering in war."

Patients, formerly victimized twice (first by a rapist, then by condescending police and pathologists), were taken immediately to the center, which was located in a trailer adjacent to the emergency room. There, they were examined by sympathetic gynecologists and received a psychiatric counseling session and routine laboratory tests before being interviewed by police. Having everything in a centralized location eliminated moving traumatized patients from one department to another and helped ensure sensitive care.

The center, renamed the Roxcy Bolton Rape Treatment Center in 1993, is open twenty-four hours a day, weekends and holidays included. By the year 2001, the center had provided care for more than thirty-six thousand victims, with chilling statistics that indicate that 65 percent were under eighteen years of age and 45 percent were under eleven years. The youngest victim was two weeks old; the oldest, 105 years.

The center tops the list of all the accomplishments for womankind attributable to Roxcy Bolton (and her dolls).

1986

Give Kids the World

Twelve-year-old Henri Landwirth raced to his father's side when Nazi soldiers burst into their home in Belgium and put a gun to his father's head. The Nazis left that day, but they returned a few months later to take Henri's father away as the boy watched, frozen in horror. Henri also endured separation from his mother and his twin sister, Margot. He suffered in several concentration camps, including Auschwitz, once jeopardizing his life for just a glimpse of his sad, skeletal mother before she was herded with one thousand other women onto a ship rigged to explode in the ocean. He suffered days without water, days with nothing but a few chunks of moldy bread, and he lived through a typhus epidemic in a room with twenty-five sick men. The men all died; Henri lived. He endured horrible atrocities, yet he lived.

In 1944, while American teenagers jitterbugged and screamed for Frank Sinatra, seventeen-year-old Henri barely survived a skull-shattering blow from the rifle butt of a Nazi soldier who left him for dead. Starving, delirious from his gangrenous head and leg wounds, he trudged several hundred miles into Czechoslovakia, searching for his sister.

Unaware that the war was ending, he was utterly without hope that life would ever change. But a voice inside repeated over and over, "Keep living . . . keep trying."

A Czechoslovakian couple found Henri asleep in a deserted building, took him in, and cared for him. After nearly losing his legs to gangrene, he recovered enough to go on looking for Margot. Hauling himself hundreds of miles to the town where he had heard Margot might be, his hopes shattered when he was told his last living relative was not there. Obeying a strange, inexplicable whim, Henri impulsively whistled a secret whistle—the twins' special childhood way to call each other. Incredibly, he heard Margot's answering whistle. She was there! "It was a gift," he said. "A miracle."

More than six million Jews died during the Nazi regime, but young Henri Landwirth and his twin sister were not among them.

Following the end of World War II in 1945, Henri returned to his native Belgium, where he worked as a diamond cutter for a few years before leaving for the United States, sailing as a deckhand to earn his way. He had a Torah, twenty dollars in his pocket, and a sixth-grade education, but he didn't have to worry about the future for long. Thanks to the US Army, Henri spent the next two years in the service, then used his GI benefits to enroll in the New York Hotel Technology School, vowing to learn the business from the ground up. He cleaned bathrooms, changed linens, and worked as a bellhop and a night clerk. Nothing was beneath him as he learned the business.

After moving to Florida in 1954, Henri managed the Starlight Motel in Cocoa Beach. The Starlight was near Cape Canaveral, where the early space program was evolving. The motel served as temporary housing for the original Mercury Seven astronauts, the military, and government contractors. As the Starlight developed into *the* place to go in Cocoa Beach, Henri formed a strong network of friendships, including the original astronauts and the famed news anchor Walter Cronkite.

Working long, hard hours, Henri managed to become a franchise owner of several hotels. As his wealth accumulated, so too did his self-imposed obligation to do good with it. The ghost of the boy who nearly starved continually hovered near the wealthy hotelier whose empathy with children was boundless. It was in his role as hotel owner that Henri discovered what he came to believe was the reason his life was spared during the dark nightmare years in Europe.

In 1986, the parents of a critically ill little girl canceled their reservation at one of Henri's Orlando area hotels. Upon investigating, Henri learned that six-year-old Amy's one wish had been to meet Mickey Mouse, but she had died before her wish could be fulfilled. Heartsick and angry that such a thing could happen to a child whose life would end before her seventh birthday, Henri learned that it usually took six to eight weeks for wish foundations to process arrangements for dying children. Six to eight weeks! Some children didn't have that long. It was something Henri had learned in Auschwitz: Every moment is precious! Someone needed to do something. Henri Landwirth stepped forward.

First Henri contacted Disney World, followed by Sea World. After that, eighty-seven Orlando hotels and the Project Mercury astronauts joined forces with Walter Cronkite and writer Art Buchwald to launch Give Kids the World, an organization designed to provide terminally ill children and their families with a free weeklong vacation near central Florida attractions. Red tape was cut to a minimum. There were no lawyers, no contracts—just Henri asking for corporate sponsors and getting them. He accommodated 320 families the first year.

On fifty-one acres of land purchased by Henri, construction of the Give Kids the World Village sprouted, nourished by volunteering individuals and corporations. Airlines provided free flights to families, who were housed in two-bedroom, two-bath villas designed to provide a breather from hospitals, medicines, and grim treatments. A beautiful promise was born: No child will ever be turned away. Families are met at the airport by greeters who help with baggage, transportation, free tickets to theme parks and restaurants, and interpreters if needed. Leaving nothing to chance, unlimited free long-distance phone service is provided at the Village to keep in touch with families at home.

When families return to the logo- and advertisement-free Village from the parks, a toy awaits each child every day. Characters from the parks visit regularly— Mickey and friends stop by every Monday and Thursday and Universal characters visit on Fridays. Christmas comes every Thursday with special gifts from Santa. The Village is magical for children, but something bewitching also seems to overtake sponsors, volunteers, and everyone connected to Give Kids the World. Their hearts are touched. Henri says, "Goodness is contagious, and it makes better everything it touches."

Parents who live with the anguish of knowing their child is terminally ill are treated to a night out during which they can reconnect with each other, but with the comfort of carrying a beeper in case they are needed.

In the Gingerbread House, families enjoy complimentary breakfasts and dinners served on furniture decorated with peppermint candies while a player piano pounds out favorite childhood songs. At the Claytonburg Park of Dreams, even wheelchair-bound guests are able to enjoy a water playground named for the Village "mayor," Clayton, a six-foot "rabbit" who visits each villa every night to tuck the children in bed. At the Castle of Miracles, a grandfather clock snores, a wishing well burps, and video games can be played for free. Guests are tempted with ice cream at the Ice Cream Palace, even for breakfast. The Amberville Train Station holds interactive trains and boats. Nature trails are wheelchair accessible, a movie theater shows children's classics, and a volunteer staff makes it all work. Medical help is always available, since the children are very sick. Sadly, some die while in Florida. As a small tribute, Village streets are named for them.

Henri, the man who started it all, looked lovingly into the children's faces and saw his own face—the boy who escaped a death-filled place to found a haven of enchantment, knowing the world is a better place because of him.

1987

Travis McGee Day

On February 21, 1987, Travis McGee Day was declared at Bahia Mar Resort and Yachting Center in Fort Lauderdale, Florida. Songs were sung, glasses raised. Copies of the book *The Deep Blue Good-by* were presented to hotel guests. A rare bottle of Plymouth gin, Trav's favorite, was given a place of honor at the Bahia Mar bar. Amid fitting revelry, slip F-18 was dedicated as a literary landmark, permanently marked with a bronze plaque in honor of the *Busted Flush* and its owner, Travis McGee. More than seventy million books relating McGee's exploits had been sold. Well-attended conferences are still held in Trav's honor. His own popular website and fan magazine further attest to his celebrity.

Who was Travis McGee? He was a deeply tanned knight without armor, carelessly clad in khaki shorts and Top-Siders, rugged and tender, softhearted and muscular, in the mold of Humphrey Bogart—tough, but with integrity.

A brief fling with football fame as a tight end concluded when Travis's legs were crushed in a bruising game, but the legs didn't stop him from serving in Korea. Except for occasional fleeting creakiness, he pretty much wiped the injury from his memory.

He lived aboard his houseboat, the *Busted Flush,* named for the poker hand in which he won it during a thirty-hour marathon played out in Palm Beach. In the final hours of the game, he loaned the big loser ten thousand dollars against the boat, and then another ten thousand dollars when that was lost, followed by the last ten thousand dollars. Finally, Travis owned the boat.

The accommodations were luxurious, if well-used. How many houseboats, even ones with a twenty-one-foot beam, can boast a shower stall nearly big enough to house a Volkswagen, not to mention a semi-sunken pale blue bathtub, seven feet long and four feet wide?

Travis tied up the *Flush* at slip F-18 at Bahia Mar Marina in Fort Lauderdale, taking pleasure in water on three sides and beneath, hearing and smelling the ocean across the street, Highway AIA. Bordering the ocean was the long, wide beach where assorted nonconformists showed off but generally minded their own business.

Travis spent his "off" hours doing odd jobs on the boat, hoping one day to trim the maintenance work to forty hours a week. When the sun set behind him, he propped his feet on the bow rail, listened to jazz, and drank Plymouth gin, while watching Fort Lauderdale's characters whiz by on boats, cars, bicycles, scooters, airplanes, and parasails.

He took jobs when the financial larder needed refilling. His line of expertise was that of salvage expert—that is, he recovered money on a contingency basis for desperate clients who had usually been cheated by confidence men. He doubted he would ever run out of work, and he never did.

When Travis needed land transportation, he bicycled to the garage where he kept his pickup truck, arguably the world's most unique vehicle—an electric blue Rolls Royce named *Miss Agnes* in honor of his fourth-grade teacher whose hair was the same shade of blue. The Rolls had been converted to a pickup by "some desperate idiot in her checkered past," but despite her age and mutilation, she purred trouble free along highways, oblivious to the stares of onlookers.

Friends sometimes compared Travis to the fictional Sam Spade or Philip Marlowe, but really good friends likened him to Robin Hood with a dash of Prince Charming. Helping damsels in distress was his specialty, but almost anyone in serious trouble who needed help—male or female—could count on Trav.

Sandy-haired, with eyes the color of blue ice, Travis sported scarred knuckles that testified to his toughness. But in truth, he liked nothing better than the long, philosophical discussions he and his boat-neighbor, Meyer, indulged in when it suited them. Meyer was a retired economist who lived a seventy-foot walk away aboard his cabin cruiser, the *John Maynard Keynes*. He was the kind of friend who actually listened, cared, and knew when to ask questions and when to keep quiet. Some of their most satisfying hours were spent ironing out the fine points of how villains had been allowed to exploit the paradise that was South Florida, whose fault it was, and how it could be prevented from happening to the rest of the state.

The exploitation of the Everglades was a large thorn in Travis's side. "Now, of course," he said in 1963, "having failed in every attempt to subdue the Glades by frontal attack, we are slowly killing it off by tapping the River of Grass. In the questionable name of progress, the state in its vast wisdom lets every two-bit developer divert the flow into drag-lined canals that give him 'waterfront' lots to sell. . . . As the glades dry, the big fires come with increasing frequency. The ecology is changing with egret colonies dwindling, mullet getting scarce, mangrove dying of new diseases born of dryness."

About the rising crime rate and loosening of the moral fiber, Trav said, "Forty million more Americans than we had in 1950. If one person in fifty has a tendency toward murderous violence, then we've got eight hundred thousand more of them now. And density alone affects the frequency with which mobs form. The intelligence of a mob can be determined by dividing the lowest IQ present by the number of people in the mob. Life gets cheaper. . . . Sociologists were orating about national fiber while every minute and every hour, the most incredible population explosion in history was rendering their views, their judgments, even their very lives more obsolete."

During a 1965 trip to Tampa and its historic cigar-making section, Ybor City, Travis said, "they are ramming the monster highways through it. . . . They've opened up the center of the city into a more spacious characterlessness, and, more and more, they are converting Ybor City into fake New Orleans. In some remote year the historians will record that Twentieth Century America attempted the astonishing blunder of changing its culture to fit automobiles instead of people, putting a skin of concrete and asphalt over millions of acres of arable land, rotting the hearts of their cities."

So why did he stay in Florida?

"Tacky though it might be," he said, "its fate uncertain, too much of its destiny in the hands of men whose sole thought was grab the money and run, cheap little politicians with blow-dried hair, ice-eyed old men from the North with devout claims about their duties to their shareholders, big-rumped good old boys from the cattle counties with their fingers in the till right up to their cologned armpits—it was still my place in the world. It is where I am and where I will stay, right up to the point where Neptune Society sprinkles me into the dilute sewage off the Fun Coast."

Travis McGee was, of course, the protagonist of twenty-one novels by John D. MacDonald, a storyteller so convincing that fifteen years after the author's death, the novels about his fictional hero, including *The Deep Blue Good-by*, are still in print. The plaque dedicated on the first Travis McGee Day is still in place on a piling at slip F-18, and Travis's bottle of Plymouth gin, sealed and reserved, is still at Bahia Mar, where he receives about a dozen letters a year from fans who refuse to believe he's no longer there, much less that he never was.

1988

A Granny Goes on Trial

Popping flashbulbs added to the confusion in the little courtroom packed with gurgling babies, squirming children, and moms waving signs reading GOD SAVE THE MIDWIVES and WE LOVE YOU GLADYS. Television camera crews and newspaper reporters shoved each other, struggling for the best vantage point.

The center of attention, tall, white-haired Gladys Milton, was plainly stunned to see so many of "her girls," their husbands, mothers, friends, and even their babies there to support her. There were so many. In almost thirty years she had helped bring more than two thousand babies into the world—every baby in Walton County in 1988—and lately she was welcoming the babies of her first babies.

She had the backing of the Florida Midwives Association and the whole Florida Panhandle, it seemed.

But in 1988, the Florida Department of Health and Rehabilitative Services astonishingly "suggested" that Gladys retire or else she would lose her license. Reluctantly, she hired Coral Gables attorney Tom Sherman, and there she was, in the middle of all the hubbub.

Gladys was a lay midwife or "granny" midwife to the state, meaning she was not a nurse and handled only low-risk pregnancies outside of hospitals. Before obstetrics became a profession, grannies delivered more than half of all babies born in the United States, until they were phased out by obstetricians. The women's movement of the 1960s and 1970s refocused attention on midwives, but registered nurse-midwives, licensed in all fifty states, gained the most. In Florida, only grannies licensed before 1984 were permitted to practice. Gladys was among the last of those women.

A central tenet of midwifery—"pregnancy is not an illness"—is disputed by many obstetricians, who cite complications that can and sometimes do occur. The National Center for Health Statistics points out that midwives have lower infant mortality rates, that their patients have fewer cesarean sections, and that technological procedures such as episiotomies, continuous fetal monitoring, and ultrasound, routinely used by obstetricians, result in millions of wasted dollars. Obstetricians maintain that these measures save lives, since their practices involve more complicated cases.

But in reality, for most of Gladys's life, hospital births were not possible for Black women (who were not admitted to White hospitals), while rural facilities were scarce for everyone.

Gladys, who was delivered by her own grandmother in 1924, learned to be a fighter early in her Panhandle childhood. Being a fair-skinned African American youngster with flaming red hair and a straight "A" average guaranteed that she stood out.

In time, Gladys married Huey Milton and had seven babies of her own, including twins, Elinor and Eleanor. As if she wasn't busy enough, she allowed the school nurse to talk her into becoming a midwife, an urgent need in Flowersview, a tiny Panhandle town.

After two years of training with two local doctors, Gladys received her license in 1959 and immediately knelt and prayed. Midwives were invariably churchwomen of fortitude and character; Gladys was no exception.

Her doctor-supervised work experience for the next five years qualified Gladys as a licensed practical nurse, and she had completed half the course work to become a registered nurse when tragedy overwhelmed her.

Her daughter Eleanor and son Kent were driving their Volkswagen home from college when they were killed by a drunken driver. Bearing the incredible agony of losing two children at once, Gladys and Huey chose to use the insurance money they received to build a small Milton Memorial Birthing Center, attached to their house.

Four months later, lightning struck and both clinic and house burned to the ground. In the confusion, a three-year-old grandson, Tyler, was forgotten until Gladys fought her way through the choking smoke to rescue him. When a patient arrived in labor, Gladys hustled her off to the nearby house of another son, Henry, who had become a physician. The indefatigable Gladys delivered the baby before dawn, graciously accepting slightly more than the customary seventy-five-dollar fee from her grateful patient, and then cooked breakfast for everyone.

With Huey's moral support and sweat equity, the center was rebuilt. Incredibly, though, two years later it burned down again due to an electrical problem. The Milton family and the community pitched in for another rebuilding, while Gladys good-naturedly suggested that maybe they should just keep everything in boxes so they'd be ready for the next time.

Gladys always believed that "babies are God's way of saying the world should go on," and go on she did, to a great honor in 1981.

That year, ten thousand babies were born in Florida unattended by medical professionals, and the legislature decided something had to be done. It set up an advisory board consisting of an obstetrician, a pediatrician, a registered nurse-midwife, and a lay midwife, Gladys Milton. The board created two schools for lay midwives, hoping to encourage women to use them rather than giving birth at home, alone. The grateful Florida Midwives Association agreed to have their patients seen and evaluated for prenatal care in hospitals.

But Gladys was noticing a change in her practice. More and more of her patients were educated, middle class, and had health insurance. Consequently, obstetricians were losing patients, and they were getting more complicated cases, resulting in more malpractice suits. It seemed no time before the previously supportive Florida Department of Health and Rehabilitative Services was recommending that Gladys's patients be hospitalized, even when they weren't having problems.

Tensions escalated when some of the same people originally responsible for encouraging the practices of midwives began undermining their work with clients. New fees were demanded, paperwork rejected, equipment improvements ordered. Gladys did her best to comply.

In 1987, a new patient arrived at her clinic, ready to deliver. She had seen a doctor just once, had no money for a hospital, and threatened to go home where she and the baby's father would deliver the baby themselves if Gladys wouldn't help. It was a case midwives were supposed to refuse, but Gladys, fearing the outcome would be worse if the woman delivered alone, couldn't turn her away. The delivery, a shoulder presentation, was extremely difficult. Despite heroic measures, the baby did not survive. Gladys unashamedly wept as she held the lifeless little body. She thought her heart would break when the mother hugged her and thanked her when the time came for her to go home.

Seven months later, Gladys received notice that her license was suspended, probably permanently. Gladys knelt and prayed, still convinced she had made the only choice she could at the time.

But rules were rules. In a jammed courtroom that resembled a daycare center, Gladys Milton went on trial for the death of that baby and thirteen other minor "infractions." When the state's attorney acerbically requested that the babies be removed from the courtroom, the judge looked around and quietly said, "They're not bothering me." A whole row of preacher-friends uttered a heartfelt, "Amen!"

During the trial, Gladys admitted to one mistake, accepting the mother of the one and only stillbirth of her career. The judge dismissed all remaining charges, but nearly two years passed before her license was returned and she finally knew she had won.

Gladys would go on to receive many awards, including Sage Femme, the highest award from the Midwives Alliance of North America. But nothing compared to delivering her first baby after the trial, when, with tear-filled eyes, she cradled the tiny child to her heart and gave thanks to God.

1988

Art Deco Queen Fights City Hall

The candlelight vigils had failed. The phone calls, the petitions, the television coverage—none of it had worked. The area around the Senator Hotel was cordoned off by authorities, but protesters managed to sneak through and chain themselves to the front door. Television cameras zeroed in on an elderly, frail-looking woman dressed in black—"robes of justice," she called them—attempting to fix a historical plaque on the white, curved plaster wall behind her. Viewers watched police drag her away before wrecking crews moved in. The Senator Hotel, L. Murray Dixon's sixty-room, spired 1939 landmark in Miami's Art Deco district, was about to be reduced to worthless rubble, ending nineteen months of struggle to keep it intact. In its place would be a parking lot.

Small wonder the woman felt faint. She suffered from diabetes and heart and lung problems. When her doctor was summoned, he hurriedly called an ambulance, suspecting a heart attack. The public relations director at the hospital, sensing an opportunity, notified the newspapers that Barbara Baer Capitman's heart was breaking. Perhaps—but not for the first time, nor the last. She could not, she would not, give up.

A journalist who worked for New York design magazines, Barbara raised two sons, and after the death of her husband, a professor at Florida International University, she reconnected with her roots at meetings with Miami designers. She recognized the riches of neglected, deteriorating South Beach, "God's waiting room," where poor retirees lived the best lives they could in their dismal, drug-infested neighborhood. The neighborhood claimed the oldest population and lowest per capita income in Florida. But Barbara admired the way the people congregated in lobbies and on the beaches, dancing, exercising, drinking coffee. She liked the way the low buildings encouraged camaraderie rather than isolation, as the high-rise condominiums the city was determined to build would do. She envisioned an architectural treasure that could be revived as a dynamic and diverse community. The obstacles would be wealthy, powerful developers, city hall, the chamber of commerce, the board of realtors, the Miami Beach planning board, and more.

The buildings, all needing costly repairs, stood on land potentially worth millions as the site of future luxurious high rises, with accordingly luxurious rents. There would be, as there already was farther north, a "Concrete Canyon," unfriendly to pedestrians, shading the beaches in early afternoon and deserted after dark. In 1976, when City Hall announced plans to bulldoze several hundred acres of South Beach, it seemed the wrecking-ball-obsessed developers had won. "Not so fast," said Barbara Capitman. Showtime!

Barbara began organizing, and with five friends formed the Miami Design Preservation League. They concocted the name while chatting on the sidewalk outside an oceanfront villa that would become infamous as the future home and site of the unfortunate demise of fashion mogul Gianni Versace. Barbara's dogged persistence secured a ten-thousand-dollar grant for a survey and plans for preservation in Miami Beach. More than twelve hundred buildings were cataloged in South Beach, most within one square mile, the largest cluster of Art Deco buildings in the world. People were starting to pay attention, to see what they had never taken time to look at before. Barbara was educating them.

But the plans of the powerful were set. According to Phase II of the development project, land west of Ocean Drive was to be sacrificed for high rises. Barbara and friends successfully pressured sympathetic officials in the Carter administration to have the district listed in the National Register of Historic Places, but that was the easy part. The state of Florida's Office of Historic Preservation, whose official approval was also needed, resisted. Powerful local interests nearly derailed the effort, but after a long, acrimonious battle, the designation was won, making the crumbling buildings eligible for tax benefits. Preservationists celebrated winning a single battle in a long war.

Using her marketing savvy, Barbara instituted the first Art Deco Weekend in 1978, a fun event designed to bring people to South Beach. A partnership headed by one of her sons bought and refurbished five hotels, opening cafes on the verandas where patrons could dine while enjoying chamber music recitals, live jazz, or recorded Frank Sinatra songs. Fashion photographers discovered the incredible South Florida sunlight, and artists moved in, including the world-renowned and eccentric artist Christo, who wrapped eleven islands in Biscayne Bay with pink polypropylene. Christo and his crew hung out on South Beach, attracting even more people to the area. A television show, *Miami Vice,* was filmed on the beach from 1984 to 1989, helping in no small way to feed the frenzy.

Still, buildings were lost. It became increasingly apparent that strong local laws were needed, since private owners could continue to demolish buildings or make inappropriate alterations. Many people were involved in the fight, but the undisputed leader was Barbara Capitman, the "little old lady in tennis shoes." She did wear tennis shoes and sacklike dresses, scarcely concerned with her appearance. Her squeaky voice and speech difficulty, plus a willful, opinionated manner, alienated people and contributed to the unfortunate impression she made. Better than anyone, she was aware of her failing health, and possibly because she knew she didn't have unlimited time in this world, she was persistent and uncompromising—to the point of obnoxiousness, some people thought. She made enemies of allies, feuding with everyone who stood in the way of preservation, even members of the Miami Design Preservation League. She was a "talkative, opinionated busybody." She "scared hell out of people." "She attacks people." These are quotes from her friends.

It was in 1988 that Barbara fought her last major battle. That was the year in which the fight to save the Senator Hotel, a privately owned jewel among the eight hundred Art Deco buildings, failed and the hotel was smashed into rubble to make way for a parking lot. By then Barbara's health was deteriorating, money troubles were mounting, and the Reagan administration had slashed funds for preservation.

However, the work never ended. New, multistory hotels were planned among the older, small ones, dwarfing them. Other inappropriate changes were being threatened, and someone had to address them. Barbara continued her work, writing a new book and learning to create press releases on a computer. Let others rest, she thought; there was too much to do. Barbara worked until the last day of her life, March 29, 1990, one week before her seventieth birthday.

Few can argue, friends or enemies of preservation, about the economic impact of the revitalization of South Beach and its spread to neighboring areas. Today, the glittering Art Deco district is one of Florida's most-visited attractions. The Art Deco Festival has grown to a weekend affair, attracting hundreds of thousands of fun-seekers. Investors have flocked to the area; property values have skyrocketed by billions of dollars. Bordering the north end of the district, formerly dilapidated Lincoln Road has been reborn into a pedestrian mall with one of the highest concentrations of art galleries in South Florida.

As Barbara herself wrote, "today, it is hard for anyone . . . to realize that in 1976 the term *Art Deco* was barely known, and that the area, so vibrant today, was considered a disgrace to the city, because of its cheap neon lights, 'funny-shaped' buildings, and the signs along Ocean Drive blaring 'rooms $5 a week.'"

In the year 2000, the Art Deco Queen was deservedly recognized as one of the two thousand deceased citizens important to the history of the state by the Florida League of Cities and the grateful State of Florida.

1990

Driving Miss Diamond

Was it life imitating art or art imitating life? Even Smiley Bruce couldn't answer that question, and he was there. In 1990, when Smiley saw the movie *Driving Miss Daisy,* he could hardly believe his eyes. It was *his* life—his and Miss Diamond's—right up there on the silver screen.

Back in 1966, Smiley, a handsome, forty-seven-year-old man, had started a new job as a driver and sort of an all-around "go-fer" for an elderly Jewish woman with the improbable name of Ruby Pearl Diamond. The relationship so closely paralleled the characters portrayed by Jessica Tandy and Morgan Freeman in the Academy Award–winning movie that Smiley said the movie was "sure enough about her and me." It was an award winner in his estimation. He loved it.

It's been said that northern Florida is the most southern part of the state and, as such, Smiley and Ruby came from entirely different worlds. Smiley, an African American who had been married to Bessie Mae Bruce since 1944, was employed full time as a night custodian. Ruby, daughter of wealthy Tallahassee merchant Julius Diamond and his wife, Henrietta, had graduated from Florida State College for Women, class of 1905. In other times, Ruby would probably have become a lawyer like her brother, Sydney, but that was not really an option for young women in the early 1900s.

For a while Ruby spent much of her time traveling, then she followed in her civic-minded father's footsteps. Julius had established the "Diamond Vegetable Basket," providing seed and fertilizer that enabled poor families to grow their own food. It was a project Ruby continued long after her father's death, just one of many ways in which she helped others to help themselves.

Ruby and Sydney both remained single and childless all their lives. A few years after their father died, they sold the family home to make way for Tallahassee's first service station. Ruby moved into Tallahassee's Floridian Hotel, remaining there for fifty years before moving to the Hilton Hotel, where she spent the last six years of her life.

When Smiley Bruce started working for her, Ruby Diamond was a seventy-nine-year-old woman accustomed to having things her way, as she'd had them all her life.

In another similarity to the movie, their relationship had a rocky beginning. Ruby was the employer, Smiley the employee. The lines were clearly drawn. For sixty dollars a week, he was her chauffeur, but he also cooked or brought her take-out meals and ran errands for her. She had rental houses that needed overseeing and occasional repair work.

Smiley supervised that work when it was necessary. Gradually, he was spending more time at the Floridian Hotel than he was at home with Bessie Mae.

In the beginning, Smiley thought Miss Diamond was prejudiced, and he was soon convinced that she didn't trust him. No matter how hard he tried, there was just no way to satisfy her. She disliked and criticized everything he did. An honest, conscientious man, he became increasingly upset and frustrated in trying to please her. Finally, as in the movie, there were one too many straws on the camel's back.

In *Driving Miss Daisy*, it was a missing can of salmon that brought things to a head. In Miss Diamond's household, the final straw came when she falsely accused Smiley of using her Cadillac without her knowledge, an impossibility since she always had the keys with her except when he was actually driving it.

Smiley talked it over with Bessie Mae, stewed about it overnight, and in the morning, with Miss Diamond sitting at her table, he poured out his frustration. He was quitting, he told her. He couldn't work for someone who didn't trust him.

Her face was an impenetrable mask as she sat silently thinking, staring first at the table, then at Smiley, then back at the table again.

At last, she pointed to a small leather bag on a wall shelf and asked him to bring it to her. It was, he knew, her collection of keys—the car keys and the keys to all her properties: apartment, bank deposit box, the other homes and properties she owned. She handed the bag to him. "Smiley," she said, "I'm depending on you to tend to all my things. What you see that needs to be done, you do." From that day on, as trust between them grew, their relationship changed from employer–employee to friends.

It was as friends that they took long drives in Miss Diamond's powder-blue 1963 Cadillac, visiting her old acquaintances or simply seeing what there was to see in the lush area around Tallahassee. Miss Diamond never seemed to tire of it. She once said, "There is no place in the world like Tallahassee. I have visited all over the world and have always yearned to return."

Although she generously gave to many causes, Miss Diamond could be tight-fisted, too, tipping waitresses sparingly and preferring to eat by the side of the road rather than patronizing restaurants, another similarity to Miss Daisy in the movie.

Smiley had to struggle for every raise over the years, but when Miss Diamond learned he was going to buy a twenty-four-hundred-dollar piano on installments, she sat down and wrote out a check for the whole amount, no questions asked—although she did mention that he didn't know how to play the piano. "I'll learn," he said.

She never criticized Smiley's driving except to repeatedly caution him to slow down. "If I slow down much more, somebody's going to run us over," he would answer.

Miss Diamond had always given generously to Jewish causes, as had the rest of her family. Following Hitler's destruction of so much of the European Jewish population, she was determined to help all she could to rebuild Jewish life, maintaining it as a priority for the rest of her life.

Spending so much time with Smiley influenced her feelings about Black people, too. One White landlord who rented houses to Black people bowed to her threats of court action by installing bathrooms in the units that previously had only outhouses. On another occasion, she paid the bail for a young Black man accused of a nonviolent crime. When holidays rolled around, she dispatched Smiley to buy restaurant meals for the needy, sometimes spending as much as five hundred or six hundred dollars.

Their relationship continued to deepen as years flew by; employer and employee became trusted friends, and in later years, Ruby thought of Smiley as her son. At one social affair he escorted her to, another guest asked her if she was with a man. She motioned to Smiley across the room. "I have one man in my life," she said. "That's him over there."

Before she died in 1982 at age ninety-five, she had a request written into her will that her most trusted friend should raise the lid of her coffin before it was buried. She wanted Smiley to be sure it was her body inside.

"When I looked in there, I went to pieces," he said. "It hurt so bad when she died."

Among the things she left him were her father's gold watch and the powder-blue Cadillac, a reminder of the years he spent driving Miss Diamond.

1992

Andrew Blows into Town

Year-round Florida residents are used to it. Along with humidity and mosquitoes, summer gives rise to television weather forecasters droning on about hurricane tracking charts, flashlight batteries, shelter locations, and disturbances off the coast of Africa. This prompts most Floridians to respond, "Africa? Puh-lease. I'm late for work." At least, that's precisely what they did in 1992—until Saturday, August 23, when Tropical Storm Andrew intensified into Hurricane Andrew and headed west, straight for Dade County.

Complacency gone, residents stood in lines for groceries and duct tape, boarded their windows with plywood, raided cash machines, gassed up cars, telephoned hotels, and tried to decide what to take if they had to evacuate. Wedding pictures? Birth certificates? Deeds to a house that might not be there when they returned? Those who stayed, hunkered down, never far from a television or radio in the eerily calm evening.

Shortly after midnight, the wind began to howl, things outside zapped and crackled, and the sky lit up a pretty, bright blue. As winds increased, anxiety levels rose. Huddled in "safe rooms," people no longer worried about property—they were fighting for their lives as they listened to nails pulling out from walls, roofs ripping off, glass shattering. Bodies leaned against walls that shook, dishes clattered in cupboards, and sewage leaked under doors. Ears popped painfully under Andrew's assault, as men braced their backs against doors trying to keep their families from being sucked from closets crammed with people, mattresses, and pillows. A few stole glimpses through peepholes, horrified to see trees and telephone poles snapped like matchsticks and cars and trucks flung like toys.

On the sixth floor of a building in Coral Gables, meteorologists at the National Hurricane Center, three of whom would lose their homes during the night, clocked winds at 164 miles per hour before the gauge broke. Fifteen-foot satellite dishes were tossed like Frisbees before the radar dome blasted from its twelve-story roost.

Torrential rains cascaded through roofs that no longer existed. Sometime around three o'clock in the morning, electric power went out, isolating people from the comforting presence of television personalities and enveloping them in blackness as seawater surged more than a mile inland. Waves flooded houses, cutting off neighbors from one another, completing the isolation.

Then after four long, agonizing hours, Andrew was gone, departed for Louisiana, where people had been watching television and most had wisely fled. Florida was left to recover.

Slowly, Floridians emerged, in shock, unable to believe what they saw. Neighborhoods had disappeared, completely erased. Devastation was beyond belief. Returning evacuees were unable to find their homes since familiar landmarks had vanished. Downed traffic lights contributed to traffic jams, escaped zoo animals were running wild, shreds of pink insulation draped crazily over everything. Fallen wires (some of them hot), rusty nails, and debris, glittering with broken glass, hampered movement on foot. Thirty-eight people were dead, and 250,000 were homeless—more than the population of St. Petersburg, Florida. Most of the survivors wandered about dazed, searching for loved ones, shelter, water, and food. They had survived a four-hour catastrophe; another longer one was beginning.

With temperatures climbing, there was no running water or electricity for ice or air-conditioning. Emergency vehicles trying to answer life-or-death calls were immobilized by debris, and the county's two rescue helicopters had been destroyed. President George H. W. Bush arrived at Opa-Locka on Air Force One and departed two hours later with promises of aid.

Although resembling a dysfunctional family before August 24, Dade County citizens, former residents of such places as Havana, Brooklyn, or St. Petersburg, Russia, connected as a community, helping each other, sharing what little they had. Those blessed with intact roofs invited strangers to sleep under them. Defrosted food from powerless freezers was cooked on charcoal grills and fed to neighbors. A man drove all the way to Georgia, loaded his truck with ice, and returned to give it away for free.

As the sounds of chain saws buzzing and helicopters thup-thupping greeted the day on Tuesday, Andrew brought out the finest in people. And the worst. Wasting no time, looters quickly emptied stores whose fronts had been ripped off. Looting for food and water was perhaps to be expected, but liquor, motor oil, and electronics went, too. One man, finding a convenience store stripped of food, took Rolaids, hoping to ease his hunger. Overworked police were spread too thin responding to life-and-death calls to stop the thievery. Signs appeared, spray-painted on shattered houses, "Looters, all good things have been removed." Guns came out of closets. With police unable to respond, every property owner with anything left seemed to be armed, on guard, and ready to shoot. South Florida needed help.

Relief efforts were in shambles, uncoordinated, snarled in traffic jams, clogged by shortened tempers fed by lack of sleep and extreme August temperatures.

By Wednesday, the County Emergency Center's director, Kate Hale, begged for state and federal aid, sadly concluding, "We've had a lot of people down here for press conferences. But . . . it is Dade County on its own." In near tears on live television, she stood up to state and federal government. "Quit playing like a bunch of kids. . . . Where in hell is the cavalry? . . . We're going to have more casualties because we're going to have more people dehydrated. People without water. People without food. Babies without formula. . . . We're about ready to drop."

But if the government was slow to respond, the rest of Florida was not. Thousands of Floridians gathered up water, diapers, and food and inched their way south on clogged highways, determined to reach suffering fellow Floridians, no matter how long it took. South Florida, land of diversity, was coming together. Police cars were loaned, portable toilets were trucked in, and volunteer medics went to work to fend off epidemics. What the government couldn't do, people did, with help trickling in from the Carolinas, Georgia, and as far north as Canada. Crews from Charleston, South Carolina, reminded of Hurricane Hugo, helped repair power lines.

Five interminable days after Andrew's visit, the "cavalry" in the form of federal troops arrived. One awestruck veteran announced, "This is worse than Desert Storm." Within two weeks, twenty-two thousand troops were deployed, making it the largest military rescue in history until Hurricane Katrina hit New Orleans in 2005. Helicopters brought supplies where traffic jams prevented it, mobile kitchens were set up and marked with helium balloons to make them easier to locate, and ten thousand radios with batteries were given out.

But recovery would be slow. Homestead Air Force Base with its eighty-seven thousand jobs was gone. Dade County's giant agricultural industry was decimated, an estimated loss of $1.04 billion. Major retail department stores and food chains lost whole stores, and one entire mall disappeared. Overall, Hurricane Andrew's toll was about thirty billion dollars, the costliest hurricane until Hurricane Katrina. Some rebuilding would take months, some years. Lessons were learned, building codes revised and enforced. Most survivors who stayed swore they would never do it again. Ever.

The good news: improved hurricane forecasting technology, giving residents more time for evacuation. The bad news: from 1960 to 1995 Florida's population tripled, and if another hurricane with the force of Andrew hits, the destruction could be even greater.

But no one should dismiss the resiliency of Floridians. Andrew had scarcely waved a final goodbye when *USA Today* carried an advertisement from the Florida Division of Tourism stating, "FLORIDA, we're still open."

1999

Right Stuff, Wrong Gender

"And we have liftoff, reaching new heights for women and astronomy!"

The words of the National Aeronautics and Space Administration's (NASA's) commentator were nearly lost as Space Shuttle *Columbia*, commanded by Air Force Lieutenant Colonel Eileen Collins, crackled and roared through NASA's glass ceiling, hurtling into the night sky over Cape Canaveral, Florida.

"You go, girl!" It was a kind of prayer that veteran women pilots and other female supporters whispered from the trembling ground at Kennedy Space Center. Eyes were glued to the fiery exhaust trail, breathing suspended, fists clenched, knuckles white.

It was July 24, 1999, almost forty years since the seven men who became this country's first space voyagers were introduced to the public. Back then, the nation was eager for heroes, tired of being beaten by the Russians ever since *Sputnik* first orbited the earth, beeping insolently with every pass. Project Mercury's pioneer astronauts were destined to become instant celebrities, heroes as familiar as movie stars, adored by youngsters, lionized by their parents. But while Project Mercury was kicked off with fanfare, another plan was launched in strictest secrecy, a classified program to determine the suitability of women for space flight.

In June 1959, Betty Skelton, a beautiful flier and champion race car driver from Florida, received notice that she had been selected to be the first woman tested by NASA. It was exciting news for someone who grew up playing with model airplanes instead of dolls, who watched naval aviators flying acrobatics from her backyard in Pensacola, and who soloed illegally at twelve years of age, then legally when she was sixteen. She became a licensed commercial pilot at eighteen and a flight instructor at twenty. Partly to ease her disappointment at not being able to ferry military planes in the Women's Airforce Service Pilots (WASP) program because she was too young, Betty took up aerobatic flying. She set so many records that she became known as the "First Lady of Firsts." But she was also first to say how lucky she felt to be able to make a career of something she loved.

Despite the thrills and excitement, Betty grew tired of the nomadic lifestyle. After returning more than one engagement ring, she recognized that she could never enjoy a normal family life if she continued the hectic schedule of air shows. So, at the doddering age of twenty-five, Betty retired from aerobatics and moved on to a more sedate realm—auto racing! She was soon setting records again.

When the call came to become the first woman tested for NASA, it must have seemed like the next logical step for a pilot with thousands of hours of flying time and one who held more aviation and auto records than anyone else in history.

For four grueling months, Betty took the same tests as the male astronauts, hoping to influence NASA to include women in the program. She learned to use an Aqua-Lung for total water immersion tests simulating the weightlessness of space and the experience of performing work in a disorienting environment. The world's largest human centrifuge whirled her at high speeds, replicating conditions under which astronauts must work. She took her turn in a high-speed rotating Barany chair, a disagreeable invention designed to convince pilots, who continue to feel a turning sensation after it has stopped, not to trust their senses but to depend on their instruments instead.

Betty scored well on all the tests, but her practical side sensed from the beginning that NASA had no intention of accepting women into the program for many years to come. While she felt honored to have played a part in space history, she was wise enough to see that it might take a lifetime for women to penetrate NASA's space ceiling. Disappointed but realistic, she moved on to marriage and an executive career in advertising, grateful for her unique experience.

Her tests for NASA, however, were the subject of a cover story in *Look* magazine on February 2, 1960. The story provoked such an outcry from other women pilots who wanted to be considered for the space program that NASA succumbed to the pressure and selected another thirteen women, who became known as the Mercury Thirteen, for testing. A heavy cloak of secrecy fell, with NASA keeping the public in the dark about the testing of women from then on.

There were some things the nation didn't learn. The women had averaged more flying hours than the Mercury Seven. One, Jerrie Cobb, logged more than ten thousand hours to John Glenn's five thousand. The women, undergoing the same tests as the Mercury Seven men, all passed, often scoring better than the men. Since the women had smaller body masses, they needed less support equipment than male astronauts did. Especially in those early days, this was an important consideration since thousands of pounds of rocket thrust was necessary for each pound of payload sent into orbit. Women were found to be less likely to have heart attacks and less vulnerable to pain, temperature changes, and loneliness. Dr. Randy Lovelace, who conducted the same tests for the women as he had for the men at the famed Lovelace Clinic, thought women were better suited than men for space travel, both psychologically and physiologically. The women even set some test records, which the men were increasingly unhappy about. So unhappy were they, in fact, that they pressured NASA to cancel the women's program.

One of the Mercury Thirteen was Jane Hart, wife of Senator Philip Hart. At his urging, a congressional investigation was launched. Included among NASA's explanations for the cancellation of the program was that pressurized flight suits for astronauts would have to be redesigned for women. Also, the men couldn't spare equipment needed to train women. However, the real catch-22 was NASA's edict that astronauts had to be jet test pilots at a time when women were not permitted to fly military jets. Since Mercury capsules were not configured anything like a jet fighter, had no wings, and had minimal controls for the astronaut, the jet experience rule was privately questioned by some experts. That the Mercury Thirteen women had thousands more hours of flying time—more than equivalent experience—did nothing to change NASA's mind. In fact, some of the Mercury Seven men even testified before Congress, saying that they thought women were not qualified to be astronauts. However, years later it was revealed that some of these same men failed to meet NASA's own requirements; they exceeded the height limit and did not possess an engineering degree. (It turns out that NASA secretly waived these requirements in certain instances.)

On June 16, 1963, Russia again beat the United States in the space race by launching the first woman in space, Valentina Tereshkova, a parachutist with no experience as a pilot. Ground controllers ran her flight from earth. Twelve years later, the Kennedy Space Center launched the first American woman, Dr. Sally Ride, a mission specialist rather than a pilot. The launch of a female pilot took another twelve years. It was a full thirty-six years from the time Tereshkova was launched to the time Colonel Eileen Collins roared into history as America's first female mission commander.

Betty Skelton, still interested in flying, space, and fast cars, was named to the Florida Women's Hall of Fame in 1993. She watched US space shots from her living room window in Florida, still wishing she could be on board, until her death at eighty-five on August 31, 2011.

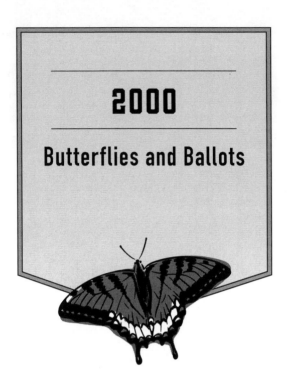

2000

Butterflies and Ballots

Massachusetts Institute of Technology meteorologist Edward Lorenz first described the "butterfly effect," the idea that a butterfly stirring the air in China in March might change the weather over the Atlantic Ocean in August. Scientists characterize the butterfly effect as the "sensitive dependence of outcomes on initial conditions." To the rest of us, it simply means the enormous, unexpected results of seemingly insignificant activities, and it must surely apply to the closest election in American history—the presidential election of 2000.

Among the "initial conditions" of the 2000 election was use of the Votomatic machine by most Floridians and by one-third of all Americans. Punch-card technology used in the Votomatic machines dated from 1890 and was so unreliable that officials had for some time acknowledged and accepted a loss of 2 percent of votes in every election due to *undervotes* (ballots with no candidate voted for) or *overvotes* (ballots marked for more than one candidate). In Palm Beach County, where a cheaper version of the problem-plagued Votomatic was in use, machines were so defective or damaged that no amount of care or intelligence on the part of voters would have prevented lost votes, regardless of disparaging appraisals by other citizens of the mental capabilities of Florida voters.

Before the 2000 election, scarcely any American had ever heard of *chads,* the tiny pieces of paper punched out by the stylus when a voter votes. After the election, most Americans learned more than they cared to know about hanging chads, dimpled chads, and pregnant chads. Few voters knew hanging chads could fall off, become stuck in vote-reading machines, or stick in other holes in the same card or in other voters' cards, causing incorrect tabulation. As far back as 1988, the National Institute of Standards and Technology urged that Votomatic punch cards be eliminated. That same year, when they were suspect in the Miami–Dade County Florida senatorial contest, voting machine manufacturers blamed election supervisors for not educating the public. Election supervisors blamed the public for making errors, while the public was unaware that special knowledge was needed to vote. One political science professor suggested that casting a vote should not be rocket science.

Other "initial conditions" affecting the outcome of the election in Florida were illegal votes cast by felons, unregistered voters who swore they were eligible but weren't, and some who voted by absentee ballot and then again in person at the polls. A large voter turnout led overwhelmed poll workers to accept a surprising number of questionable votes. When workers sought help, they faced jammed phone lines at election supervisors' offices.

Furthermore, the workers were put to work after only four or five hours of training and were paid minimum wages to work long, grueling hours. Many were elderly, sometimes frail, but were usually principled, honest, and patriotic.

As long as a year before the 2000 election, another "initial condition" originated with Florida Governor Jeb Bush's "One Florida Initiative," a program that ended affirmative action in granting state contracts and in higher education. By failing to consult with Black leadership and refusing to meet with Black legislators on the matter, the governor so aroused the ire of African American Floridians that they turned out in record numbers to vote against his brother in the presidential election—60 percent more than had voted in 1996. The problem was that many were first-time voters and no one had shown them how to vote. Most refused to ask for help; some did and were rebuffed by poll workers. Additionally, many new Haitian American citizens had language difficulties that hampered their ability to vote correctly. Accusations of unauthorized roadblocks by police in Black voting districts surfaced and were denied, causing Jesse Jackson to fly into the state to rally his people, convinced they were being disenfranchised.

Probably the most significant "initial condition" came into existence when, six months before the election, an average person in a boilerplate job—the Palm Beach County supervisor of elections—began preparations for the 2000 election. She was responsible for staffing 531 precincts, training four thousand poll workers, checking qualifications of candidates, and, despite having no training in the field, choosing the ballot design. The design that was approved quite likely tipped the balance in votes in the county and was considered by some as the most important component in installing the man who lost the popular vote into the highest office in the nation.

The unusually large number of presidential candidates on the ballot—ten in all—would have been crowded on a one-page ballot, requiring type that Palm Beach County Supervisor Theresa LePore considered too small for the large elderly population to see easily. Instead, she chose a design with the candidates' names split on two pages. With that small action, the butterfly ballot was born—the butterfly flapped its wings, stirring the air toward enormous, unantic-ipated consequences.

In fairness, candidates, political party bosses, and the general public were shown the ballot, and no complaints were registered. The problem was that the ballots as shown to all those people did not show the punch holes between the two pages, which was exactly what many found confus-ing when confronted with the real thing. George W. Bush's name topped the left page, with Albert Gore's just below. Pat Buchanan's name was on the right page, between the two, which meant that although Gore's name was second from the top of the page, the hole that had to be punched for him was third from the top. Had the ballot been user-tested, which it was not, its flaws would have been apparent immediately. As such, the poor design of the ballot was a most import-ant "initial condition" affecting the extraordinary events that followed. By 9:00 AM on election day, phones in LePore's office started ringing. By 10:30, people were arriving in per-son, all complaining about the ballot, some in tears.

After comparing notes with neighbors, many elderly Jewish voters suspected or knew they had mistakenly voted for Buchanan, whom they perceived to be an anti-Semite. Buchanan, the Reform Party candidate, had accumulated such an amazing number of votes in the Jewish community, one resident said, "Yasser Arafat could have gotten more votes here." A rabbi added, "If Palm Beach is a Buchanan stronghold, then so is my synagogue." People in their eighties—some Holocaust survivors who had waited all their lives to vote for a Jewish candidate—knew their vote for Joe Lieberman, Gore's running mate for vice president, was lost.

LePore's reaction? She understood that the ballot might have caused some confusion, she said, but voters needed to take some responsibility.

Then the race for the presidency came down to a dead heat. Just a few hundred votes would decide the election in Florida and—because of the state's large number of electoral votes—in the nation. For thirty-six days, Americans watched the two main political candidates mount claims and counterclaims, file suits and countersuits, and issue challenges and demand recounts in a bizarre display of political science that ended with the decision of the US Supreme Court in favor of George W. Bush.

Have the butterfly wings stopped flapping? Hardly. Historically, just one new life-tenured presidential appointee to a sharply divided US Supreme Court can profoundly influence the direction of the country for many years beyond any president's administration. The fundamental rights of all citizens are affected by far-reaching judicial decisions.

Additionally, the presidential election of 2000 led to the realization that the voting process in the nation is terribly flawed. Florida led the way in replacing unreliable voting

machines, redesigning ballots, and retraining poll workers and their supervisors—part of a decade-long process to
upgrade voting equipment and procedures nationwide in
order to carry out the will of the people.

The gentle wings of the butterfly ballot continue to flap.

2001

Space Chimps Retire

In the mid-1950s, the US Air Force authorized hunters to capture sixty-five baby chimpanzees from the wilds of Africa. Knowing that a strong mother-infant bond existed, hunters first stalked and then killed the mother chimpanzees before tying the screaming babies to poles and carrying them to the coast, where they were crated and shipped across the ocean. One out of ten chimps survived to arrive in the United States, where the Air Force took control of them. Experiments began, some spinning the unfortunate babies in giant centrifuges to test their reaction to enormous G forces, others measuring the length of time it took before the chimps lost consciousness in a decompression chamber.

To determine whether mental facility would be affected by conditions during space launches, weightlessness, and reentry, the chimps were rigorously trained and tested using a system of rewards and punishments for performance on a simulated panel with levers and lights. Correct responses earned banana pellets; incorrect ones brought a mild electrical shock to their feet.

By 1961, NASA was ready. On January 31, a three-year-old chimp named Ham was strapped onto his couch in the Mercury capsule. After a six-hour delay, the enormous Redstone rocket rumbled and roared into space, almost immediately malfunctioning. The capsule, expected to travel at forty-two hundred miles per hour, instead reached fifty-eight hundred miles per hour, exposing Ham to 18G forces, instead of 11Gs, as had been predicted. Ham, however, performed his duties perfectly, returned to Earthly applause and was featured on the cover of *Life* magazine. Three months later, human astronaut Alan Shepard followed Ham into space.

To get a capsule into orbit was another matter, requiring a more powerful rocket. Testing the new Atlas rocket, five-year-old chimp Enos, first in his class, was launched on November 29, 1961. After numerous glitches during lift-off and a shaky first orbit, several malfunctions caused the cabin temperature to rise and fuel usage to increase rapidly. The capsule wobbled and the reward-punishment system flipped into reverse. The "dumb beast" who had trained for more than a year should have performed incorrectly due to the topsy-turvy delivery of banana pellets and shocks. But Enos did what he knew was right, despite receiving a shock for every correct move he made. The third orbit was aborted. Enos was saved from certain incineration when he was removed from the capsule, which registered 1061 degrees Fahrenheit.

NASA made 250 adjustments to the spacecraft based on what was learned during the Ham and Enos flights. John Glenn was launched ten months later.

While some chimps were not trained for flight, all were tested in painful, frightening ways to gauge the dangerous or unpleasant effects encountered in space travel.

Human astronauts became instant heroes, to an extent that surprised even NASA. Ticker-tape parades, television interviews, lucrative offers, and adoration were showered on the Mercury Seven while the "chimponauts" were reassigned to "hazardous mission environment"—testing seat belts. Then in 1970, the Air Force began leasing the chimps out for biomedical research that involved infecting them with AIDS or hepatitis. That was eventually determined to be useless since chimps reacted differently than humans. In the meantime, however, another group of former space chimps had their teeth smashed in with a steel ball to provide experience in reconstructive procedures for dental students. The chimps, social animals who live in groups and have a life span of fifty years or more, were housed in too-small cages, denied access to outdoors, companions, or diversions of any kind.

According to famous primatologist Jane Goodall, "Research shows that chimps think, feel, and communicate in ways almost identical to man." She has proven that they use tools, have emotions, and play with toys. They kiss, embrace, and have a dark side, as humans do.

Seventy years ago, about one million chimpanzees lived in the African wilds. There are perhaps 150,000 left there today. Estimates of chimps in the United States range from 1,300 to 2,000. Of those, decreasing numbers are housed in research facilities as retired chimps are moved to sanctuaries, while others remain in zoos or kept as pets—a sad fate for our closest living relatives, who share all but 1.4 percent of our DNA.

Protests by Goodall and Roger Fouts, pioneer of chimpanzee language research, and John Glenn, former astronaut and senator from Ohio, went nowhere. Instead, the Air Force transferred the chimps to the Coulston Foundation, an organization with laboratories in New Mexico, which had already been investigated twice for negligence, including two gruesome deaths.

At that point, Carole Noon arrived on the scene. Noon was a former student of Goodall's, whose trip to Africa in the 1980s inspired her to become a wildlife biologist. During a lecture by Goodall at Florida Atlantic University, Noon decided to work with chimps. It was a good fit from the start. She and the chimps enjoyed each other's company. The animals played tricks on her and laughed when she fell for them. They inspired her admiration for the way they triumphed over the degradations they suffered at the hands of humans.

Noon had just finished working in Africa on the project for her doctorate—mixing chimps orphaned by poachers with foster parent chimps to form families—when she heard about the space chimps being turned over to the Coulston Foundation, which had been accused by the US Department of Agriculture of mistreating 650 of its chimpanzees.

Reacting swiftly, Noon petitioned that the chimps be awarded to the Center for Captive Chimpanzee Care. She was the founder of the organization but unfortunately as yet had no facility in which to house the animals. Although she had enlisted Goodall and Fouts to serve on her board of directors and speedily raised nearly two million dollars, the Air Force still refused to give her the chimps because she had no permanent place to put them.

By securing the backing of thirty-five members of Congress and the Doris Day Animal League, plus a gift of one million dollars from the Arcus Foundation, Noon bought 150 acres of a Fort Pierce, Florida, orange grove, where she proceeded to have an island with jungle gyms and two houses for the chimps constructed while she sued the Air Force for custody. After a tough, year-long court battle, she won custody of twenty-one of the chimps and moved to a trailer on her land in order to oversee the completion of a refuge for the Air Force retirees.

The first US sanctuary devoted exclusively to permanent lifetime care of chimpanzees had begun, and Carole Noon was on her way to providing a secure, enriching habitat where the chimps could live a life similar to what their lives would have been had they never been taken from their homes.

When the first eleven of the space chimps arrived in their new Florida home in mid-April 2001, Noon expected some of them would have psychological problems. However, after being torn from their mothers, crated and shipped to another continent, spun, squeezed, bashed, and put in solitary confinement, the chimps looked around and settled in quietly. They must surely have felt as though they had been released from a house of horrors. A second group followed two months later and, to Noon's amazement, reacted the same way.

Still, they were born and raised in captivity. They must live in separate cages, separated by mesh, until they become acquainted with each other, a long process that cannot be hurried. Slowly, the chimps begin learning to be chimps again, playing, grooming, brawling, and making up.

More chimps arrived as they became expendable to researchers or difficult to handle for entertainment. They form families, but they will not have families. Males are sterilized. "A sanctuary's goal should be to go out of business solving problems created by someone else," Noon said.

Meanwhile, the notorious Coulston Foundation was investigated by several independent government bodies, found to have repeatedly violated regulations, and charged four times with violating the Animal Welfare Act. The charges included the negligent deaths of ten chimpanzees. Additionally, Coulston faced having its research invalidated by the Food and Drug Administration for repeated violations, and it lost vital funding from the National Institutes of Health. The bankrupt lab closed in 2002, transferring the care of 266 chimps to Dr. Noon's organization, Save the Chimps, which provided care and improved conditions at the New Mexico facility while gradually moving the chimps in a custom-built trailer, a few at a time, to Florida.

Save the Chimps has grown to be one of the world's largest chimpanzee sanctuaries, with twelve separate three- to five-acre islands where chimps form families and are free to roam, play, and socialize. In order to maintain their peaceful lives, the facility is not open to the public.

On May 2, 2009, after a brief illness, the chimpanzee's friend, hero, and next-door neighbor, Carole Noon, died at her home in the paradise she built for them. The work she dedicated her life to will go on.

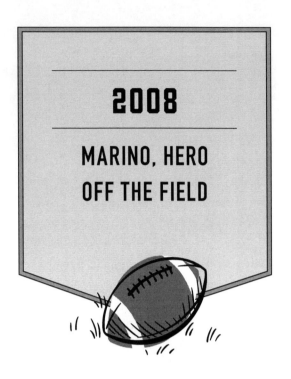

2008

MARINO, HERO
OFF THE FIELD

He spent his boyhood in Oakland, a blue-collar section of Pittsburgh, in the shadow of University of Pittsburgh's Cathedral of Learning, where all the parents looked out for all the neighborhood youngsters. At the time, there were just three television channels, no internet, no PlayStation. The noise of marching bands and exuberant fans filled the air every Saturday afternoon in the fall when the Pittsburgh Panthers played at home, ensuring that sports were an important part of boys' lives.

The brick row houses had backyards too small to play ball, but the boys used the streets for baseball in the summer and football in the fall. Telephone poles were end zones, and curbs were out of bounds as they dodged cars and buses and snow or piles of autumn leaves, depending on the time of year.

Dan Marino's dad, coach of a semipro league, gave pointers to his son on how to throw a football, which was what Dan wanted to do—throw a football. He worked hard to achieve the lightning-quick release that would one day be famous. Dan never wanted to play any position but quarterback, and though he would never be renowned as a scrambler, his ability to avoid the pass rush might be the result of the hours he spent jumping rope on the roof of his parents' flat-top garage after the other boys went home. Much later, he realized that while his dad was teaching him to pass, he was also teaching him to be a man.

His football skills were impressive very early on, so much so that his grade school's football field was named the Dan Marino Field before he moved on to high school. His outstanding record in his senior year of high school led to his being selected for the *Parade* magazine High School All-America team, and his jersey, number 13, was retired when he graduated. The Kansas City Royals drafted him to play baseball, but Dan elected to stick with football in his hometown. He passed on baseball and on a chance to play football for Notre Dame or the University of California, Los Angeles.

The University of Pittsburgh Panthers played their home games right there in the Marino neighborhood, guaranteeing that Dan had his own special cheering section. While he worked toward a bachelor of arts degree in communications, he had a spectacular college football career, establishing records for pass attempts, completions, yardage, and touchdowns, all with family and friends looking on.

Disappointed that he threw too many interceptions in his junior year, he knew it was important not to allow such things to undermine his self-confidence, but he didn't forget them either. The year after Penn State defeated the Panthers

48–14, ruining Pitt's chance for an undefeated season and a national title, Dan frequently wore a T-shirt with "48-14" on it at practices, reminding himself of his own fallibility.

He earned first-team All-American honors in his junior year. The following year, he was inducted into the College Hall of Fame, his number 13 jersey was retired, and he was drafted by the NFL's Miami Dolphins. Though his senior college year had been a disappointment, he later considered it a blessing to have been passed over by twenty-six teams in the draft because it led to his being picked for the Dolphins by Don Shula, launching an extraordinary thirteen-year relationship. The two men would go on to win more games than any other coach/quarterback duo in football history.

Dan's first year as a Dolphin was so impressive, observers wondered if he could get any better. In his second season, he did get better, and quarterback records fell like autumn leaves. His strong, bullet-like passes were so phenomenal, medical writers tried to figure out why. Having started his NFL career by being named Rookie of the Year, he went on to be inducted into the Pro Football Hall of Fame and named the Most Valuable Player, AFL-AFC Player of the Year, and All-Pro eight times, plus too many other honors to relate here.

Teammates said he was so good at passing the football, he could do it if he were semiconscious, which he apparently proved during a game in 1992 when he was blitzed so hard by offensive linemen that, he needed help off the field. After sitting out one play, he went back into the game, still woozy from a concussion, and threw the winning touchdown pass.

In 2000, after seventeen years as a Miami Dolphin, Dan Marino gave up the game he loved. The Dolphins retired his number 13 jersey, and the grateful city of Miami changed

199th Street, which leads to Pro Player Stadium, to Dan Marino Boulevard, where a life-size statue of its hero was erected.

As much a hero as Dan was to sports fans for a big part of his life, he became even more of a hero to countless other people whose lives he has touched, either through his and his wife's philanthropic efforts or simply by helping children struggling with serious health problems, visiting them in hospitals, hugging them, or sending gifts to encourage them.

His parents had always believed in the importance of family. Dan's father delivered newspapers and worked odd jobs to support the family, while no sacrifice was too much for his mother to provide for Dan and his two sisters. Friends were always welcome at the Marino home. Pitt Panthers frequently showed up for spaghetti and meatballs at the Marino house after college games, and neighbors opened the gates between their small backyards to accommodate the young people.

In 1985, Dan married his college sweetheart, Claire Veazey, and as time passed the couple welcomed sons Daniel Charles, Michael Joseph, and Joseph Donald, and daughter Alexandra Claire. Later, two daughters, Niki Lin and Lia, were adopted from China.

When their second son, Michael, was almost two years old, he didn't cry much, didn't interact with his brother at all, and didn't try to talk. The pediatrician wasn't concerned, but Claire and Dan suspected something might be very wrong. They sought help from a program for children with developmental delays, and that's when Mikey was diagnosed as having autism.

The diagnosis of autism is a shock in any family. Mothers and fathers wonder what they did to bring on such a challenge, and then most seek to learn everything they possibly can to help their child. Success and fame doesn't change that; Claire and Dan reacted as any other parents would.

They started Mikey on intensive therapy, working with a parade of therapists every day. The Marinos hired speech therapists, occupational therapists, physical therapists, one-on-one teachers—still, it wasn't until Mikey was four years old that his parents began to see signs of improvement. Progress was slow, but by the time he started third grade, Mikey could be enrolled in some mainstream classes. He continued improving, and long before he entered college, few people meeting him for the first time suspected he had ever been diagnosed as autistic.

Claire and Dan realized how fortunate they were to be able to afford the expensive therapies Mikey benefited from, and they knew many parents were not so lucky. In 1992, they created the Dan Marino Foundation to support autism research, including clinical studies and training focused on its causes and treatment.

Knowing the difficulties of having various services spread out in many locations, sometimes miles apart, Claire and Dan joined with Miami Children's Hospital in 1998 to create the Nicklaus Children's Hospital Dan Marino Outpatient Center in Weston, Florida, near their home. The pediatric center provides diagnosis and treatments and has come to serve approximately thirty thousand children each year.

In 2005, the foundation established the Marino Autism Research Institute (MARI), which supports researchers, clinical service delivery, and education under the combined auspices of the University of Miami and Vanderbilt University in Tennessee.

While Claire and Dan continue to help raise millions of dollars for other families, their son Mike knows how blessed he was to have made such a remarkable recovery and is determined to follow in his parents' footsteps, helping other people like himself.

Dan became a father again in 2005 and he admitted to having had an affair with a colleague to whom he paid much money to keep silent about it. Though he maintained contact with the baby and spent millions to support her and the mother, he and his wife stayed together.

He issued a statement saying, "I take full responsibility both personally and financially for my actions now as I did then. We mutually agreed to keep our arrangement private to protect all parties involved. My wife and I have been married for almost thirty years and have six children together. And we continue to be a strong and loving family."

In a short time, the mother of the child married and had a child with her husband.

A Dolphin for seventeen years, Dan often met with dying children after the games. He visited them in hospitals with hugs, gifts, and smiles. He never hurried them, never checked his watch, and always asked, "Is there anything else I can do for you?" before he grinned, said goodbye, and then escaped to nearby hallways to fight the tears.

He was proud to stand beside Charlie Crist in 2008 when the Florida governor signed into law a bill requiring large insurance companies to cover treatment for children with autism.

"It's a very proud day for me to be a Floridian," Dan said.

Florida is proud of Dan Marino, too.

2008

LONG LIVE THE CONCH REPUBLIC

The agreeable citizens of Key West concurred once more. Although the Conch Republic Independence Celebration had been celebrated for twenty-six years, everyone agreed the week-long party in April 2008 was the best one ever, and as everyone knows, if there's one thing the people of Key West know how to do, it's party.

The fanciful-but-true story of how in 1982 Key West seceded from the Union, formed the Conch Republic, declared war on the United States, surrendered, and wasted no time requesting foreign aid has been cause for annual merrymaking ever since.

It all started on the afternoon of Sunday, April 18, 1982, on the mainland, just south of Florida City, directly across from the Last Chance Saloon, supposedly in response to a growing drug problem. US Border Patrol agents, brandishing shotguns, joined stone-faced troopers from the Florida Highway Patrol in setting up a roadblock, complete with flashing lights and undercover Drug Enforcement Administration (DEA) agents lurking in the background, on US Highway 1, the only road to the Keys. Not only did the Feds begin demanding proof of US citizenship, they thoroughly searched each vehicle and every passenger for illegal substances.

"All of those tourists covered with oil" were stopped and searched as thoroughly as though they were returning from a foreign country. Not surprisingly, the broiling sun did its work on drivers and passengers as the lines grew longer and people sweltered for as long as five hours in a twenty-mile pileup. Tempers flared, and bottles and whatever else was handy were turned into projectiles aimed at law enforcement officers, while some drivers illegally sped north on the shoulders of US 1 or on the nearly empty southbound lanes, making impolite gestures through their car windows. The fun-filled weekend was history.

Pouncing on the story, the media reported that a border checkpoint had been set up within the United States and the Keys were being treated like a foreign country. As always, bad news traveled fast, so that before night fell most of America was aware of the ugly situation in the Sunshine State. At that time of the year, with the slower summer season coming on, most visitors to the Keys were South Floridians who drove in on US 1, with the result that cancellations of hotel and room reservations came in at dismaying rate. Tourism *was* the Key West economy.

Dennis Wardlow, the mayor of Key West, put calls through to Florida's governor, senators, and congressmen, to Robert Adams, the border patrol chief in Miami, and to Vice

President George H. W. Bush, who was then the head of the Reagan administration's Task Force on South Florida Crime. Most of those called responded by agreeing to "look into it," except for Adams, who, alluding to the nation's growing drug problem, affably promised he would continue having cars stopped "seven days a week, twenty-four hours a day."

Key West residents and officials fumed. Not only was the tourist industry being adversely affected, they said, but with so much publicity, every drug smuggler and illegal alien in the hemisphere knew enough to avoid northbound US 1 out of the Keys. So what was the point?

Responding to escalating demands from residents of the Keys and to heated discussion among city officials, a local attorney was hired to file an injunction against the US government in federal court in Miami.

It was a good try, but the court refused to order the border patrol to end all of the roadblocks. Instead, while not admitting to any of the allegations put forward by the Key Westers, the authorities announced they would allow a normal flow of traffic to resume and intermittently stop just a small number of cars to check identification. They would conduct searches only if there was probable cause.

The delegation from Key West was not mollified. Even the modified checkpoint was an insult to the citizens of the community. Key West was not a foreign country!

When Mayor Wardlow left the courthouse, he confronted the horde of reporters and television cameras at the door. Waving the Key West flag he had with him, he informed the crowd that at noon the next day, Key West would secede from the Union and become the Conch Republic.

Back home in Key West, the mayor assured irate members of the community that, contrary to a report in the *Miami*

Herald, under no circumstances would the Stars and Stripes be lowered. Instead, the Conch flag would be raised beneath it. Key West would secede from the Union, he said, but it would be a *mock* secession.

At high noon on April 23, 1982, Mayor Wardlow and a group of supporters climbed aboard a flatbed truck in Old Town Square, surrounded by a typical Key West crowd—that is, folks in T-shirts, bathing suits, and flip-flops, drinking Cuba Libres and waving signs advising DON'T TREAD ON THE CONCHS and REMEMBER THE ALOE.

The mayor first proclaimed his love for America, emphasizing once more that it was a *mock* secession, but declared that if the politicians in Washington were going to treat Key West like a foreign country, the community was left with no choice.

Amid applause and cheers, the blue, pink, and yellow flag of the Conch Republic was raised on a flagpole near the truck. Mayor Wardlow, who had morphed into Prime Minister Wardlow, shouted, "Long live the Conch Republic!"

When the cheering died down, the Conch Republic's minister of defense, also a plumbing contractor, took the microphone, proclaiming to the crowd that he was declaring war and a takeover of the territorial waters of the Conch Republic. An unsuspecting US naval officer in the crowd was invited to join the officials on the truck, but when he did, he was attacked by the minister of defense—with a loaf of stale Cuban bread.

It was war.

The minister of defense then handed the bread to the navy officer, saying, "We surrender."

When the cheering crowd quieted down, Prime Minister Wardlow took over. He proudly announced that the Conch Republic had seceded, fired a shot, surrendered, and was now applying for foreign aid.

Summer arrived as it always does, and with the temperature soaring, the annoying roadblock gradually fizzled, disappearing without fanfare during a night in June, but word about the plucky little republic had begun to spread. As it did, the annual Conch Republic Independence Celebration grew from a one-day party to a week-long event, getting bigger and attracting more people every year.

The festival begins with the Raising of the Colors at Fort Taylor, followed by a picnic and obligatory kickoff party, complete with a conch shell–blowing contest at the Schooner Wharf Bar.

A highlight of the week is the "World's Longest Parade." Although not measured in miles, the parade does begin at the Atlantic Ocean and wind its way to the Gulf of Mexico, boasting in-line skaters, quirky floats, musicians, decorated bicycles, and visiting firemen.

Probably the most famous event of the week is the Conch Republic Bed Race, in which four-wheeled beds are decorated and occupied by one team member while four others push the beds down Duval Street. Prizes are awarded, and money is raised for charity.

On another day, a naval battle pits the Conch Republic Navy against the Feds in the form of the Coast Guard, firing everything from water guns to Cuban bread to juicy fruit and overripe vegetables.

There are shell-blowing contests, pedicab races, a car show, fiddler contests, and poetry slams, and there are parties, of course—often before, usually during, and always after each event.

The important thing, the Conchs believe, according to a recent press release from the Conch Republic's secretary general, is: "As the world's first fifth-world country, we exist as a state of mind, and aspire only to bring more warmth, humor, and respect to a planet we find in sore need of all three."

In 1986, a small monument was erected in front of the chamber of commerce, dedicated to the heroes of the Conch Republic. They have not yet received the one billion dollars of foreign aid they requested in 1982, but they haven't given up hope. So far, the United Nations has ignored the Conch Republic's application for admission.

Word of the Independence Celebration spread, and inevitably, other celebrations were added. Before long, Key West hosted "The World's Longest Party" and found almost any other excuse for a party that anyone could dream up. Tourists flocked.

The Conch Republic issues impressive-looking passports and visas, which, according to reports, have been honored in Canada, thirteen Caribbean countries, France, Russia, Spain, and Ireland.

Some important resolutions have been issued, establishing the following:

Official drink: Cuba Libre

Official weapon: Bread, stale

Official foods: Conch chowder, conch fritters, key lime pie

Unofficial song: Jimmy Buffett's "Margaritaville" (another official song was written, but it was considered far too somber)

Official motto: "We seceded where others failed."

First announced foreign policy: "The mitigation of world tension through the exercise of humor."

Long live the Conch Republic!

BIBLIOGRAPHY

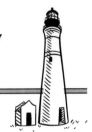

General Sources

Gannon, Michael. *Florida: A Short History.* Gainesville: University Press of Florida, 1993.

Kleinberg, Eliot. *Florida Fun Facts.* Sarasota, FL: Pineapple Press, 1995.

Ponce de León's Reception in the New World

Davis, T. Frederick. "History of Juan Ponce de León's Voyages to Florida: Source Records." *Florida Historical Quarterly* 14 (1935).

Derr, Mark. *Some Kind of Paradise.* Gainesville: University Press of Florida, 1998.

Fuson, Robert H. *Juan Ponce de León and the Spanish Discovery of Puerto Rico and Florida.* Blacksburg, VA: McDonald and Woodward, 2000.

Peck, Douglas. *Ponce de León and the Discovery of Florida.* St. Paul, MN: Pogo Press, 1993.

Tebeau, Charlton. *A History of Florida.* Coral Gables, FL: University of Miami Press, 1971.

Osceola Betrayed

Hartley, William, and Ellen Hartley. *Osceola: The Unconquered Indian.* New York: Hawthorne Books, 1973.

Seminole Tribune, Hollywood, FL, June 18, 1999.

Ward, May McNeer. "The Disappearance of the Head of Osceola." *Florida Historical Quarterly 33,* nos. 3–4 (1955).

Wickman, Patricia. *Osceola's Legacy.* Tuscaloosa: University of Alabama Press, 1991.

Dr. Gorrie Makes Ice

Gladstone, John. "Cool It, Said John Gorrie." *South Florida History Magazine,* Spring 1996.

Howe, George D. "The Father of Modern Refrigeration." *Florida Historical Quarterly* 1 (1909).

Jahoda, Gloria. *The Other Florida.* New York: Scribner, 1967.

Barefoot Mailmen

Castello, David J. "The Barefoot Mailman." *Boynton Beach Times,* Boynton Beach, FL, October 1997.

Oyer, Harvey E., III. "The Barefoot Mailman." *South Florida History* 28, no. 4 (Fall/Winter 2000).

Pierce, Charles. *Pioneer Life in Southeast Florida.* Coral Gables, FL: University of Miami Press, 1970.

Pratt, Theodore. *The Barefoot Mailman.* Port Salerno, FL: Bemis, 1993.

A Question of Courage

Peters, Thelma. *Lemon City.* Miami, FL: Banyan Books, 1976.

Straight, William M., MD. "The Lady Doctor of the Grove." *Journal of the Florida Medical Association* 56, no. 8 (August 1969).

Henry Flagler's Divorce

Akin, Edward N. *Flagler: Rockefeller Partner and Florida Baron.* Gainesville: University Press of Florida, 1992.

Chandler, David Leon. *Henry Flagler.* New York: Macmillan, 1986.

Martin, Sidney Walter. *Florida's Flagler.* Athens: University of Georgia Press, 1949.

Tampa Nurse Builds a Hospital

Adams, John Henry. "The Clara Frye Hospital." In *The Negro Blue Book of Tampa,* circa 1925.

Brady, Rowena. *Things Remembered: An Album of African Americans in Tampa.* Tampa, FL: University of Tampa Press, 1997.

Colburn, David R., and Jane L. Landers, eds. *The African American Heritage of Florida.* Gainesville: University Press of Florida, 1995.

Tampa Morning Tribune, Tampa, FL, April 9, 1936.

Tampa Tribune, Tampa, FL, July 8, 1990.

Tampa Tribune-Times, Tampa, FL, February 26, 1989.

A Chinese Man's Faith in America

Furnas, J. C. *The Americans.* New York: Putnam, 1969.

McCunn, Ruthanne L. *Chinese American Portraits.* San Francisco, CA: Chronicle Books, 1988.

Murry, Marian. *Plant Wizard: The Life of Lue Gim Gong.* New York: Macmillan, 1970.

Press Journal, Vero Beach, FL, May 13, 2001.

Weaver, Brian, and Richard Weaver. *The Citrus Industry.* Charleston, SC: Arcadia, 1999.

Carl and His Elephant

Foster, Mark S. *Castles in the Sand.* Gainesville: University Press of Florida, 2000.

Redford, Polly. *Billion-Dollar Sandbar.* New York: Dutton, 1970.

Marjory's Poem

Carper, N. Gordon. "Martin Tabert, Martyr of an Era." *Florida Historical Quarterly* 52 (1973).

Douglas, Marjory Stoneman. *Voice of the River.* Sarasota, FL: Pineapple Press, 1987.

Eckert, Edward. "Contract Labor in Florida during Reconstruction." *Florida Historical Quarterly* 47 (1968).

Powell, J. C. *The American Siberia.* Gainesville: University Press of Florida, 1976.

A Black Town Destroyed

Dunn, Marvin. *The Beast in Florida: A History of Anti-Black Violence.* Gainesville: University Press of Florida, 2013.

González-Tennant, Edward. "Remembering the Rosewood Massacre." JSTOR Daily, January 1, 2023. https://daily.jstor.org/remembering-rosewood-massacre/.

Jones, Maxine D. "The Rosewood Massacre and the Women Who Survived It." *Florida Historical Quarterly* 76, no. 2 (1997): 193–208. https://stars.library.ucf.edu/fhq/vol76/iss2/7/.

Saving Betty Mae

Jahoda, Gloria. *Florida: A Bicentennial History.* New York: Norton, 1976.

Jumper, Betty Mae. *Legends of the Seminoles.* Sarasota, FL: Pineapple Press, 1994.

McCarthy, Kevin. *Native Americans in Florida.* Sarasota, FL: Pineapple Press, 1999.

Seminole Tribune, September 11, 1998.

Nazis Invade Florida

Farrant, Don. "Up Periscope." *Florida Living Magazine,* February 1999.

Forum, The Magazine of the Florida Humanities Council 22, no. 3 (1999).

Huckshorn, Robert J. *Government and Politics in Florida.* Gainesville: University Press of Florida, 1991.

Kleinberg, Eliot. *War in Paradise.* Melbourne: Florida Historical Society Press, 1999.

Prior, Leon O. "Nazi Invasion of Florida." *Florida Historical Quarterly* 49, no. 2 (October 1970).

A Quiet Hero

Green, Ben. *Before His Time: The Untold Story of Harry T. Moore, America's First Civil Rights Martyr.* Gainesville: University Press of Florida, 2005.

Marquette, Gregory. *The Bomb Heard around the World: The Lives and Deaths of Harry T. and Harriette V. Moore.* Ft. Lauderdale, FL: Top Cat II Production Publishing Group, 2019, c2017.

Saunders, Robert W., Sr. *Bridging the Gap: Continuing the Florida NAACP Legacy of Harry T. Moore, 1952–1966.* Tampa, FL: University of Tampa Press, 2000.

A Small Patch of Cuba

de Quesada, Alejandro M. *Images of America.* Charleston, SC: Arcadia, 1999.

Greenbaum, Susan D. *Afro-Cubans in Ybor City.* Tampa: University of South Florida, 1986.

Harner, Charles E. *A Pictorial History of Ybor City.* Tampa, FL: Trend Publications, 1975.

Hewitt, Nancy A. "Varieties of Voluntarism: Class, Ethnicity, and Women's Activism in Tampa." In *Women, Politics and Change.* New York: Russell Sage Foundation, 1990.

Mormino, Gary, and Anthony Pizzo. *Tampa: The Treasure City.* Tulsa, OK: Continental Heritage Press, 1983.

Poyo, Gerald E. "A Woman's Place in Building a Grass Roots Victory." *Forum* 18, no. 2 (Summer 1995).

Cuban Missile Crisis

Florida Times-Union, Jacksonville, FL, October 4, 1997; January 20, 2001; January 21, 2001.

Kennedy, Robert F. *Thirteen Days.* New York: Norton, 1969.

National Security Archives, Washington, DC, August 2, 2001; August 30, 2001.

Orlando Sentinel, Orlando, FL, January 12, 2001.

Time, November 2, 1962.

Dr. Cade Wins the Orange Bowl

"Father of Gatorade and Wife Fund Professorship." *Florida Physician,* Fall 1999.

"Fifty People Who Made a Difference: Robert Cade." *Gainesville Sun,* July 6, 2001.

University of Florida Oral History Program. Transcript of interview with Dr. Cade. Received December 13, 2000.

Tired Housewife from Micanopy

Audubon News, Florida Audubon Society, October 10, 1997.

Carr, Marjorie Harris. "A Florida Scandal." Florida Defenders of the Environment, November 1996.

Derr, Mark. *Some Kind of Paradise.* Gainesville: University Press of Florida, 1998.

"Fifty People Who Made a Difference: Marjorie Carr." *Gainesville Sun,* October 8, 2000.

Monitor 18, no. 3 (Winter 1999); 19, no. 3 (Fall 2000).

Ocklawaha River Restoration, History of Restoration Efforts. Florida Defenders of the Environment, November 28, 2000.

How the Mouse Got His Kingdom

"Empire of the Sun." *U.S. News & World Report,* May 28, 1990.

Fogelsong, Richard E. *Married to the Mouse.* New Haven, CT: Yale University Press, 2001.

Frearson, Steve. *A History of the Walt Disney World Resort.* Burbank, CA, 2000.

Orlando Sentinel, Orlando, FL, December 16, 2001; December 17, 2001; December 18, 2001; December 19, 2001.

Walt Disney World. Walt Disney Productions, 1981.

The Last Straw

Florida State Archives. Roxcy Bolton Collection, Series 1394, Carton 22, and Series M94-1, Carton 2.

Miami Herald, Miami, FL, February 28, 1984; October 18, 1988; November 9, 1990; May 9, 1994; December 10, 1998; August 27, 1999.

New York Times, September 11, 2000.

Give Kids the World

Landwirth, Henri. *Gift of Life.* Privately published, circa 1996.

Los Angeles Times, October 15, 2000.

Lowe, Cindy. "Give Kids the World!" *Florida Living Magazine,* October 1988.

Travis McGee Day

MacDonald, John D. *Bright Orange for the Shroud.* New York: Fawcett Crest, 1965.

——. *Darker Than Amber.* New York: Fawcett Crest, 1966.

——. *The Deep Blue Good-by.* New York: Fawcett Crest, 1964.

Merrill, Hugh. *The Red Hot Typewriter.* New York: St. Martin's Press, 2000.

A Granny Goes on Trial

Bovard, Wendy, and Gladys Milton. *Why Not Me?* Summerton, TN: Book Publishing Company, 1993.

DeFuniak Herald, DeFuniak, FL, June 24, 1999.

Griffin, Katherine. "Gladys." *Health Magazine,* May/June 1992.

National Center for Health Statistics. Press release, May 19, 1998.

Susie, Debra Anne. *In the Way of Our Grandmothers.* Athens: University of Georgia Press, 1988.

USA Today, November 10, 1995.

Art Deco Queen Fights City Hall

Capitman, Barbara Baer. *Deco Delights.* New York: Dutton, 1988.

Capitman, Barbara Baer, Michael Kinerk, and Dennis W. Wilhelm. *Rediscovering Art Deco USA: A Nationwide Tour of Architectural Delights.* New York: Viking Studio Books, 1994.

Miami Herald, April 1, 1990.

New York Times, February 7, 1988.

O'Connor, Lona. "The Queen of Art Deco Fights On." *Historic Preservation,* September/October 1989.

Wisser, Bill. *South Beach: America's Riviera, Miami Beach, Florida.* New York: Arcade, 1995.

Driving Miss Diamond

Memorial program. *Dedication of the Diamond Family Social Hall,* February 22, 1985.

Photocopies from the Ruby Diamond Collection at Florida State University Library, Tallahassee, FL, June 1, 1967.

Tallahassee Democrat, March 11, 1990.

Transcripts of interview with Ruby Diamond. Florida State Archives, April 18, 1970.

Andrew Blows into Town

Kleinberg, Howard. *The Florida Hurricane & Disaster 1992.* Miami, FL: Centennial Press, 1992.

Miami Herald Staff. *The Big One: Hurricane Andrew.* Miami, FL: *Miami Herald,* 1992.

Moore, Marilyn A. "After the Big One." *South Florida Magazine,* October 1992.

Staff of *Sun-Sentinel,* Fort Lauderdale, FL. *Andrew!* Orlando, FL:
    Tribune, 1992.

Right Stuff, Wrong Gender

America's Sports Car. Bowling Green, KY: National Corvette
    Museum, June 3, 2001.

Cooper, Ann. "Betty Skelton: An Exceptional Woman." *Woman
    Pilot Magazine,* September/October 1998.

Correspondence from Betty Skelton Frankman to author, June 12,
    2001.

Florida Today, June 21, 1998.

Holden, Henry M. "Women in Space—the Mercury 13." *World
    Airnews,* August 1999.

Look, February 2, 1960.

Steadman, Bernice Trimble. *Tethered Mercury.* Traverse City, MI:
    Aviation Press, 2001.

Butterflies and Ballots

Correspondents of the *New York Times. 36 Days.* New York: Times
    Books, Holt , 2001.

Gleick, J. *Chaos.* New York: Penguin, 1997.

Linder, Doug. "Of Ballots and Butterfly Wings." University of
    Missouri-Kansas Law School, November 15, 2000.

Miami Herald Staff. *The Miami Herald Report.* New York: St.
    Martin's Press, 2001.

Washington Post Staff. *Deadlock.* New York: PublicAffairs, 2001.

Space Chimps Retire

Center for Captive Chimpanzee Care Newsletter 1, no.1 (Fall 2000)

Fort Lauderdale Sun-Sentinel, January 31, 2001.

Fort Pierce Tribune, February 9, 2001.

Las Vegas Review Journal, August 7, 1998.

National Geographic News, August 6, 2004.

New York Times, Obituaries, May 7, 2009.

Orlando Sentinel, July 31, 2001.

Palm Beach Post, March 15, 2001.

Save the Chimps. savethechimps.org.

Marino, Hero Off the Field

Fedele, John. "Pitt Alumnus, Football Hall of Famer Dan Marino to Deliver Pitt's 2008 Commencement Speech." *Pitt Chronicle,* newspaper of the University of Pittsburgh, Pittsburgh, PA, April 14, 2008.

Fiedler, Tom, ed., staff of the *Miami Herald. Marino: Stories from a Hall of Fame Career.* Chicago, IL: Triumph Books, 2005.

Glazer, Jay, SportsLine Senior Writer. CBS Sports NFL. November 30, 2002.

Marino, Dan, with Steve Delsohn. *Marino!* Chicago, IL: Contemporary Books, 1986.

Mitchell, Houston. "Dan Marino Fathered a Child with CBS Employee in 2005." *Los Angeles Times,* January 31, 2013.

Today Show. "The Marino Family's Fight against Autism." MSNBC .com. February 22, 2005.

Long Live the Conch Republic

Keith, June. *Key West & the Florida Keys.* Key West, FL: Palm Island Press, 1997.

King, Gregory. *The Conch That Roared.* Lexington, KY: Weston & Wright. 1996.

Secretary-General of the Conch Republic. *The Conch Republic.* Key West, FL: Key West Web Services, 1996–2004.

INDEX

ABOUT THE AUTHOR

A former Pennsylvanian now residing in Vero Beach, Florida, a lover of books and history, **E. Lynne Wright** was a nurse anesthetist, wife, and mother of three before embarking on a writing career. Since then, her short stories, nonfiction articles, essays, and book reviews have appeared in the *Cleveland Plain Dealer, Hartford Courant, Mature Lifestyles, Woman's Day,* and numerous anthologies and literary magazines. Exploring Florida by land and boat has inspired a love for the state's natural beauty, its people, and its history. Lynne is also the author of *More than Petticoats: Remarkable Florida Women* as well as *Disasters and Heroic Rescues of Florida, Myths and Mysteries of Florida: True Stories of the Unsolved and Unexplained, Speaking Ill of the Dead: Jerks in Florida History, Florida Disasters: True Stories of Tragedy and Survival,* and *Florida: Mapping the Sunshine State through History* (coauthor).